"We need to talk"

Tough Conversations with Your

Boss

"We need to talk"

Tough Conversations with Your

Boss

From Promotions to Resignations
Tackle Any Topic with Sensitivity and Smarts.

LYNNE EISAGUIRRE

Avon, Massachusetts

Published by
Adams Media, an F+W Media Company
57 Littlefield Street, Avon, MA 02322. U.S.A.
www.adamsmedia.com

ISBN 10: 1-59869-881-8
ISBN 13: 978-1-59869-881-7

Printed in the United States of America.

J I H G F E D C B A

Library of Congress Cataloging-in-Publication Data
is available from the publisher.

This publication is designed to provide accurate and authoritative
information with regard to the subject matter covered. It is sold with
the understanding that the publisher is not engaged in rendering legal,
accounting, or other professional advice. If legal advice or other expert
assistance is required, the services of a competent professional person
should be sought.

—From a *Declaration of Principles* jointly adopted
by a Committee of the American Bar Association
and a Committee of Publishers and Associations

Many of the designations used by manufacturers and sellers to distinguish their product are claimed as trademarks. Where those designations appear in this book and Adams Media was aware of a trademark
claim, the designations have been printed with initial capital letters.

This book is available at quantity discounts for bulk purchases.
For information, please call 1-800-289-0963.

Contents

Acknowledgments

As I finish this, my fifth book, I realize that teams, not just authors, produce books. I am grateful for my own dream team. I'm indebted to my agent, Michael Snell, who came to me with the proposal for this book. Chelsea King at Adams Media created the original concept, and helped me shape and refocus the content, while remaining cheerful and optimistic—everything a writer wants in an editor. Brendan O'Neill served as additional and useful support.

On the home front, my hard-working and upbeat assistant, Shannon Duran, typed and proofed endless versions of this book without complaint. Val Moses offered last-minute editing. I'm thankful to many clients who trusted me with their personal stories. Their names and identities have been changed in many situations to protect the innocent.

Friends Bill Cahal, Susan Hazaleus, and Val Moses helped shore up my attitude. My fellow "villagers," residents of my co-housing community in Golden, Colorado, offered in-the-trenches training on the realities of creating productive conversations and dialogues instead of debates.

My parents, Joe and Wilma Eisaguirre, and siblings, Kim Jones and Lew Eisaguirre, provided moral support and their usual unflagging belief in my abilities—as well as teaching me much of what I know about difficult conversations! (That's a joke, guys!)

On the home front, Nancy Fox helped care for my children with devoted attention so that I would have the time and energy to work. John Evans provided moral support as well as extra child care. And of course my kids, Elizabeth and Nicholas, worked cheerfully on their own books so that I would have the time to write mine. I love you more than any writer's words can ever express.

Introduction

You're beating budget. You're on schedule. You've been complimented on your outstanding work. You've done everything your boss has asked, and more. Life is good, except for the fact that you've got insomnia. Sweaty palms. A knot in your stomach. It's all because you're worried about having a conversation with your boss about upgrading your title and salary.

How is it that we human beings struggle so much with talking about what's important to us? On the one hand, it's hard to believe that there are so many competent, articulate, well-educated, intelligent, creative, talented people working in the world who fear conversation more than almost any other situation. On the other hand, it's not difficult to imagine at all. From entry-level workers to front-line managers to CEOs, I have worked with people at all levels of organizations to help them develop the skills to have successful conversations about challenging topics. The truth is that even veteran managers and senior leaders struggle with discussing issues such as complaints, performance issues, and other workplace woes. If *they* have problems, it's normal that you would feel intimidated also.

Do you know how to break difficult news to the boss, ask for a raise, a bonus, or a break? Do you know how to find out how you're really doing and ferret out the unwritten rules of your workplace? Do you wish you had a career coach and a script to use as a model to start a tough conversation?

Disagreeing with your boss isn't inherently stressful. You can root for rival baseball teams and even make a friendly little bet on the outcome. You can disagree about whether a high-protein diet or just controlling food portions is a better way to manage your weight. But when there's something at stake, watch out. When the topic is whether you get a promotion, the opportunity to lead a project, or time off to care for an ailing parent, there are tangible outcomes riding on the dialogue. If your manager's perspective doesn't align with your own, it can hinder your ability to carry on an intelligent, calm conversation.

Given our opposable thumbs, ingenuity, and capacity for emotion, the human response to stress seems less impressive than one might expect. What's up with that? After millions of years of evolution, it's a little disappointing that we still experience a primitive "fight or flight" response to duress. But it's there and it's hard-wired into the human brain. Under stress, the body goes into high gear in a hurry. Your heart rate goes up, your pupils dilate, your system is flooded with adrenaline and cortisol, and blood moves away from the digestive tract to your muscles and limbs so you are ready to flee or fight. No wonder it's so hard to communicate when you feel stressed. Your body is poised for action, not dialogue.

What's in It for You?

Your stress is about to go way down. *We Need to Talk: Tough Conversations with Your Boss* is like having a support team on call 24/7. This book is a step-by-step guide through the most common difficult conversations that employees inevitably need to have with their bosses. Based on thousands of consultations, negotiations, and speaking engagements, the best-practice advice here will give you the words and tools you need to navigate workplace conundrums with grace and success.

As president and CEO of Workplaces That Work, I speak several times a month throughout the United States to groups of 20 to 2,000. These groups span the spectrum of hourly employees to executives. I've spoken to truckers and travel editors, factory workers and farmers, attorneys and astronauts. They all share common dilemmas: what to say at work when they don't know what to say.

I spent several years as an employment attorney before becoming a consultant. I've litigated cases and continue to advise clients through my consulting practice about how laws impact everyday workplace interactions and conversations. If you follow the advice and rules outlined in this book, you'll learn how to know when to talk and when to stay silent. You'll be equipped with great opening lines and "tee-ups" to a conversation; you'll be able to recognize when to cut your losses and leave the room, when to speak up, and when to be silent. You'll also learn the art of breaking down difficult conversations into bite-sized pieces so you don't swallow the thing whole, but manage it in small bites.

A Disclaimer, Since I'm an Attorney

If you have an HR (human resources) department or director in your organization, it's always a good idea to try to seek their advice or counsel. If you use this book before you talk with them, it will give you a general idea of what to say—and perhaps more important, what not to say—but it can't give you the specifics on your organization's policies and culture, which can be critical. Don't overlook these important nuances. Your HR department wants you to have a successful relationship with your boss and you can often benefit from spending time with an HR professional before you talk with your boss.

Of course, there remain certain circumstances where you'll need to consult an attorney, regardless of the tools in this book. This book is not meant to be legal advice: that can only be gained through a consultation with your own attorney and by developing an attorney-client relationship. The information here is offered for educational purposes only. What this book may do, however, is help you decide when you need to consult an attorney and when you can go it alone. *This book is not a substitute for competent legal advice.*

Boss Communication Don'ts	Boss Communication Dos
Avoid conflict.	Embrace conflict as a call to change.
Take your boss's behavior personally.	Depersonalize your boss's behavior.
Rely on outdated skills or instinct.	Learn conflict and communication skills.

"We need to talk"

Chapter 1

How to Find Out about the Realities of Your Job

JOEL SAMPSON LEANED back in his chair and closed his eyes, but the job specifications swam in his head anyway. On the one hand, there was that list of goals in his job description that included specific objectives he was supposed to accomplish in order to get an outstanding rating on his annual performance review. On the other hand, his boss seemed to have priorities that did not really line up with the detailed list of objectives outlined in the written job description.

It was clear that he needed to talk to Kyle, his boss, but that was nearly impossible. Kyle was a platinum-level frequent flyer, jumping on and off planes around the globe, meeting with clients and making deals. When he was in the office, it seemed that there was a perpetual line of people waiting for him outside his office door. Even if he could find a free spot on Kyle's calendar, Joel had absolutely, positively no idea what to say!

Managing Up

Your boss is not the only person with management responsibilities. You have them, too. It's true, even if you do not have a single staffer reporting to you, your success is tied to how well you manage your boss. This idea, called *managing up*, is a proactive approach to working with your boss to achieve the best outcomes. Translation: you win, your boss wins, and your organization wins. Managing up is really the only viable long-term strategy for a successful relationship with your boss. Hating your boss gets you nowhere fast. Kissing up only gets you somewhere for a limited time. Managing up will yield sustained good things for you and your boss.

Regardless of your job description, managing your boss is actually one of your primary responsibilities because your relationship with your boss is invaluable to both of you. You are mutually dependent on each other. Your boss provides direction, feedback, resources, and support (or not, if you have an incompetent boss).

Your boss also depends upon you. Your boss looks to you to produce great work, solve problems, find inventive solutions, collaborate with others, and contribute to achieving organizational goals.

If you do not engage with your boss regularly, you won't be in a position to get what the boss has to give.

Get to Know Your Bosses

First things first. In most organizations, you have more than one boss. Often there is a single boss who is in charge of your performance appraisal, but that person usually relies on feedback from other leaders to give you an accurate appraisal. It is likely that you will find yourself working on a variety of projects, led by different people who all play a role in how you move up the ladder. Moreover, you may have to have a challenging conversation with a project leader, who may or may not be your direct manager, and you will need to navigate that relationship with as much skill as you communicate with your main boss.

Regardless of how many bosses you really have, you don't have a lot of time and neither do those bosses. So, invest some time upfront to get to know them. You need to understand what makes them tick, what they want, what their strengths and weaknesses are, what pressures they feel, and what their career goals and aspirations are. If you can discover those, you can find out how to support them in their mission. This will help keep you from spinning your wheels and guessing what they want. Exploring these topics will allow you to think about your bosses in a much more dynamic and multidimensional way. You will find commonalities and connections you did not know you shared, and this will enable you to interact more productively and enhance your relationship. For instance, you may discover that the reason one of your bosses never seems to get back to you in a timely manner is that he absolutely prioritizes answering voice mails over e-mails. All those comprehensive e-mails you have been sending regarding important projects are sitting in his in box, idling away because he can never seem to get to e-mail the way he zips through voice mail. If you start calling him, you will get better results. Remember, the goal isn't communicating in the manner you prefer; the goal is getting your ideas heard and your questions answered.

The Really Important Stuff

Managing up takes a high degree of emotional intelligence and patience. You need to prioritize this over your job description, the department's goals and objectives, and your organization's vision, which are important, but irrelevant to this discussion. Your job description becomes quite simple once you understand your bosses' priorities and goals. The bottom line is that you have to understand what it is that your bosses want for themselves. Even if your boss is incompetent, it is still important. If you're lucky, you will only have one or two incompetent bosses to contend with, but believe me, you are better served to have them be grateful and incompetent than agitated and incompetent.

Say, for example, you know that your direct boss wants to be the next vice president of development. You need to know what she needs to accomplish that goal. You need to understand what lies between her current spot and that vice-presidential office. That gap is laden with opportunity for you! If you understand what the missing pieces are and can become a valuable ally in completing the puzzle, you're well on your way to increasing the value of your own stock.

Know your bosses' idiosyncrasies. If your supervisor values punctuality, beat expectations by showing up early. If your boss places a premium on structure, make sure you send a detailed agenda ahead of meetings. This is not rocket science; in fact, a good deal of it is common sense and effort.

How to Get the Lowdown

There are ways to get any information handily. There is, of course, the time-honored method of asking the office know-it-all.

"We need to talk"

Try this little exercise as a litmus test for how well you know your boss. Take a piece of paper and make three columns with these headings: values, fears, and needs help. Now, think about your boss and see if you can come up with ten things your boss values, ten fears your boss has, and ten items with which you could help your boss. If you struggle to come up with three or four, you have work to do!

Every office has a person who seems to have the inside scoop on everything. It could be a long-time employee at a low-level job in the mailroom. It might be an administrative assistant or a mid-level employee who seems to befriend everyone. It may not be the person in your group with the most power, but the person bursting with the most information. You might get some inside information by simply asking. Usually those people love to answer such questions because they relish being in the know. Try asking. You never know unless you ask. It is also a good place to practice your communication skills, as there is really nothing at stake.

A much more efficacious choice would be to go straight to the source: your boss. Ask your boss to go to lunch, have coffee, or meet for a drink after work. As a rule, bosses respond very favorably to such requests. They like the initiative it shows and the opportunity to connect with their staff. Do not sit around waiting for your phone to ring, expecting your boss to call you and invite you for coffee. If you are feeling overworked, so is your boss. Your boss has more worries, deadlines, and responsibilities than you do. Does it mean you should refrain from asking, since your boss is so busy? Absolutely not! It simply means that your boss is likely to be preoccupied with a myriad of other things. That said, your boss is very likely to welcome your outreach.

Remember, the objective of a more casual get-together with your boss isn't to accomplish a litany of items on your own to-do list. It's to get to know your boss. Find out a bit about her professional journey, how she got where she is, what she loves about her current job, where she sees herself in a few years, and what does she do to refuel and re-energize herself for the demands of the job. All these topics will give you insight into your boss's personal aspirations and priorities. Understanding your boss is one of the best investments you can make in your own career.

If you are more introverted and the idea of having lunch is intimidating, start with a simple cup of coffee. It's more informal and takes less time. If your boss is the opposite gender and you're concerned about appearances, invite a colleague to join you. Regardless of whether it is coffee or lunch, or even a drink after work, end the experience by thanking your boss for the time and indicate that you would like to get together regularly so you can stay connected. Your boss is likely to be receptive and will be grateful for your foresight. Many bosses routinely tell me that it is refreshing and appreciated when employees suggest informal gatherings; regardless of how busy they are, they want to make room in their schedules because they also find them valuable.

Ask and You Shall Receive

Managing up is not always easy, but it is always worthwhile. In addition to getting to know your bosses, you need other information so you can do your best work and reap the rewards of your blood, sweat, and tears. You know the old adage—never assume anything. Never is that more relevant than with bosses and kids, and sometimes it's hard to distinguish between them! Do not, for a second, presume that you know your boss's expectations. When you were hired, your boss may have given you some guidelines around expectations, but that was then and this is now. Sweeping generalizations about the need to perform at a high level and be held accountable for outcomes doesn't give you enough information to perform well or achieve outcomes.

You need clarity, and the only way to get that is to ask for it directly. You are not supposed to magically discern this yourself by osmosis. If you think just hanging out and observing is going to give you the Holy Grail, you are wrong. Only your boss can give you the map to the treasure. Do not hesitate for a minute. Do not think that your boss will think you're incompetent if you ask. In fact, your boss will begin doubting you if you don't ask! Take the lead. Initiate dialogue with your boss to clearly outline deliverables. You need to know precisely what the objectives are and then reconfirm them in writing. Having a written record of the agreement regarding objectives and priorities helps keep both of you focused and on track. It will also help you if things change, and it is entirely possible that there will be a 180-degree turn on some goal or priority. It happens all the time.

In a global economy, the markets shift instantly, a major opportunity could appear out of nowhere, or a hot prospect could disappear in an instant. You cannot blame your boss. You have to be light on your feet, keep your finger on the pulse of the industry, and stay in touch with your boss. The more proactive you are in communicating, the better the result. Dash off a quick phone call or e-mail to your boss, thanking him for new information or input, and be positive about embracing the change. Even the most jaded bosses appreciate enthusiasm.

If the new information creates a significant problem, tackle it directly. Suppose a new product launch is pushed forward so your company can be first to market. It is up to you to have a frank dialogue about what compromises might need to be made in order to launch early. Maybe quality will suffer. Maybe the project will be over budget because overtime is required to meet the new deadline. You need to help your bosses adjust their expectations in situations like these. It is always beneficial to spell out any trade-offs that have to be made when there's a change in course; you want your bosses to know what the stakes are so they can make an informed choice.

Why Bosses Don't Spell It Out

If you were a mind reader, your job would be infinitely easier. Absent that, it would be great if bosses simply made their goals and objectives clear. Why don't they? There are many reasons.

Time Crunch

The number one reason bosses do not do so is that most would need to clone themselves to be everywhere they are supposed to be and do everything they're supposed to get done. The demands on them are enormous. Smartphones and wireless technology have only amplified the problem, not cured it. Bosses are chronically bombarded in an electronic paper chase. Most senior executives get over a hundred e-mails per day. Add to that double-booked meetings and a plethora of phone calls, and there is no time to do any work. Breathing barely fits into their schedules! With that kind of pressure, it's a rare gem of a boss who can pause long enough to mentor you and assist you with priorities.

Too Many Demands

Similarly, some bosses have too many people reporting to them, making it impossible for them to remember details related to each staff person's work and what the problems are to offer guidance on. They might be great bosses simply spread too thin. You can easily help yourself here. Give your boss a break by feeding her updates on these topics regularly. Just give a concise, no-nonsense, objective progress report. Think of it as an "elevator meeting." You have two minutes on the elevator with your boss to provide keen insights, discuss how you're handling obstacles, and give a relevant summary of progress. Your boss will appreciate it.

Warm and Fuzzy—Not

Some bosses may also simply lack people skills. Companies whose success rests on innovation place enormous value on people who can solve technical problems. They have amazing IQs. Despite all that intellect, they lack the ability to manage people and rarely get the training they need to become better managers. Hence, management is populated by people who are brilliant but managerially inept. Whenever an organization values technical competence so disproportionately over leadership and communication abilities, disaster looms. Eventually, tensions will mount until a crisis explodes, wreaking havoc on an organization and its most talented people.

For example, Phil took over as the general manager of a chain of retail stores after an extensive interview process with the owner and the owner's business coach. Phil was warned that the boss—although a technical expert—had "poor people skills" and needed help in that area. Despite that admonition, Phil took the job and spent his first three weeks on the job doing low-level tasks. He didn't spend even a single hour with the owner. There was no "welcome to the company" lunch, no kick-off meeting or significant orientation beyond what every new employee received from human resources. Phil had no idea what he was really supposed to do, how success would be measured, or what the long-term strategy for the company was. He busied himself doing tasks that really should not have been his job, but they occupied his time, and he was grateful. Finally, with no interaction forthcoming from the owner, Phil decided to leave. He wanted a boss with better management skills. He wanted to learn from someone. He also wanted feedback about how he was doing, where they were headed, and more. He wanted a relationship with his boss.

Sometimes Your Boss Doesn't Know Either

Sometimes a boss simply has no idea what to do with you. This could be because she hasn't been given much direction, because the company is undergoing turmoil, because she inherited you from someone else, or for any number of other reasons. Although it is not pretty, if the boss doesn't know what to do with you, she can't communicate her needs to you. As frustrating as it is, sometimes a manager does not have the skills or the energy to do anything different. Don't be discouraged by that though. This is just an opportunity in disguise. If you take the lead on communication and defining your role, you could have yourself your dream job!

Bad Bosses

It is also possible that you simply ended up with a bum boss. Your boss may be incompetent. Incompetent bosses happen to good people, no question. Your boss is your boss for one very important reason: someone above him thinks that he should be the boss. He may have worked, bribed, slipped, or sidled his way to the top, but the fact that he is managing you is not necessarily a reflection of his skills and ability. It is merely a reflection of what is. Whining about this sad (but common) state of affairs will not help you.

All of the reasons why bosses don't communicate are fairly benign. That is not the case if you have a "devil incarnate" (or DI) boss. This is a boss from hell. Think of a gangster. Think of the Meryl Streep character in the hit movie *The Devil Wears Prada*. Some such bosses relish making their underlings look like fools. They may have character defects or real psychiatric issues, but whatever the reason, they appear to enjoy making you look stupid and/or setting up artificial tests for you to pass. If you find yourself working for such a boss, you have limited options. Those bosses are very unlikely to change or become more compassionate. You will need, instead, to focus on learning what you can from them while you plot your escape to your next job. Managing such a boss can be the ultimate challenge in managing up.

Unless your boss is doing something illegal, immoral, or fattening, there are no real "bad bosses," just those you're not managing well. Understand that managing up is on your job description, no matter whom you work with, and sharpen your skills in this area.

Ideally, you would find out all this about your job before you're hired or promoted. There's one key question you should ask at the interview stage: query the interviewer about a typical day, hour by hour. If he can't give you that information, that alone will tell you a lot. If he seems stumped, ask to speak to someone who is currently doing the job or a similar job. Someone should be able to give you the hourly play-by-play. This synopsis will go far in giving you the realities of your job.

Asking: Specific Requests That Get Results

It is established that managing up requires asking your boss questions. Without fail, the question I always I get from my clients is how to ask questions. Although whatever you want to ask may seem daunting, it's much easier if you use a specific method I call "1-2-3 Go!"

First, before you begin the challenging part of the conversation, always start by establishing rapport with your boss. This is true regardless of whether you have a great, close relationship with your boss or not. You build rapport by talking about easy topics first. You ease your way into the delicate topic. You do not want to walk into your boss's office and unceremoniously blurt out news. This is called "teeing up" the conversation.

In golf, before you launch a beautiful drive down the middle of the fairway, you step into the tee box, look down the fairway, plan your approach, and take a few warm-up swings. Then you place the ball on the tee, focus, keep your eye on the ball, and use your best swing, transferring energy from the club head to the ball so it soars exactly where you want it to go. Use that same system in a conversation. Use a brief "tee-up" before you delve into delicate topics. Good tee-ups include questions or statements about the weather, company news, local sports teams, an item on display in the boss's office, or a generic question about the family.

> ### "We need to talk"
>
> Do not ask questions about specific family members unless you know the individual members quite well. The last thing you want to do is inadvertently bring up a painful topic like a divorce or a death.

After a few minutes of easy small talk, it's time to get to the challenging topic. This is where the 1-2-3 Go! format will help you make the request gracefully. The idea is that you sandwich the challenging request in between more comfortable remarks of understanding or appreciation. Here is how it works:

1. Offer understanding or appreciation.
2. Make a specific, doable (something they can say or do) request.
3. Add more appreciation or understanding.
4. *Go!* Do not hover, nag, apologize, equivocate or whine! Go!

Here is an example of a common situation. Suppose you have a boss who doesn't seem to give you any meaningful feedback about your future. You want to walk out of your boss's office with a tangible result, but the result you receive isn't the feedback you want. As much as you may want that, approaching your boss without warning isn't going to give you the kind of feedback you want. If you have not been getting that, asking your boss when your boss has no idea the question is coming won't do it. You will be frustrated and you will have thwarted your own goals. Instead, make a specific request around the topic that is doable. Your conversation would go something like this:

1. I understand how busy you are, and I know that everyone seems to need a piece of your time.
2. I'm wondering if we could spend some time together, perhaps having lunch one day next week, so we could talk about my place in the department. (Boss agrees, checks calendar and sets a date.)
3. I appreciate your taking this time to talk to me about my career.
4. *Go!* This is when you leave.

In the previous example, you articulated your needs and you gave your boss a way to say yes without putting him on the spot. You didn't require that he answer your question then and there. What you accomplished was even better; you got him to commit to a conversation about the topic on a specific date and time. Now, when you do meet, your boss will be prepared to give you meaningful feedback.

Most people are not in the habit of making specific requests. Instead of making a request, they lodge a complaint! That's a dreadful strategy and predictably unproductive. Furthermore, most people don't even complain to the person who can do anything about the problem. Instead, most people whine to a colleague, their best friend, spouse, therapist, or priest. Make it a habit to avoid whining, and talk to the person who can actually do something about the problem. A good mantra to use whenever you hear yourself complaining is to say something like "Wow! I could have made a request."

Sample Script

"We need to talk"

Here's an example played between Joel and his boss, Kyle. This takes the example and makes it concrete. See if you can spot each part of the 1-2-3 Go! format.

JOEL: Kyle, I'm wondering if you have a minute to talk about something. I know how busy you are but I need to schedule a specific time to talk about my place in our group. (That was 1: Understanding and appreciation.) Could you please try to see if you could find some time on your calendar this week? (Number 2: Specific request.)

KYLE: How about after this phone call I have to take? I'll be free in just a few minutes. Sit down—this will just take a minute.

JOEL: Ah . . . sure.

KYLE: What's up?

JOEL: I've been looking at the work that I've been doing for you and going over my job description. I realize that there always needs to be flexibility in any project but I'm not clear about whether my thinking is aligned with yours. I want to talk about that.

KYLE: Well, I'm not exactly sure what you mean but perhaps . . .

JOEL: What I mean is that I am not sure that the things I'm actually spending most of my time on line up with what you want and with my job description. I realize that job descriptions are not an exact blueprint of what every person does, and of course, they can't possibly cover everything. But still, I'm not sure what I'm doing will accomplish your goals and objectives.

KYLE: Could you be more specific?

JOEL: Sure. For example, my job description says that I'm supposed to assist the department in reducing error rates on orders, but I just

16

never get the feeling you're terribly interested in that. Do you have any ideas on how I could be more useful in that arena?

KYLE: I wasn't even aware that was in your job description, but no, I wouldn't say that would be the primary thing. We actually do pretty well in that area. A while back, we had some issues there, so that may be why it's in everyone's job description, but you don't really need to worry about that.

JOEL: Great, that's very helpful to know that. If you could name one thing that you would find most useful for me to spend my time on, what would that be? (Specific request.)

KYLE: That's easy—talking to new client leads. I never have enough time for that, and with our department goals this year, we need to generate leads that are more viable.

JOEL: I can definitely do that. I really appreciate your taking the time to talk to me about this. (Appreciation.) I feel so much clearer about what I should be doing. Thanks so much.

KYLE: No problem.

Boss Communication Don'ts	Boss Communication Dos
Stay in the dark about your boss's goals.	Gather intelligence about your boss's aspirations, fears, and areas needing most assistance.
Wait for your boss to tell you what is important.	Be proactive in communicating with your boss.
Complain to others.	Ask your boss where you should focus your energies.
Talk in generalities.	Make specific requests of your boss.

Chapter 2

How to Challenge a Bad Performance Review

KAREN HERNANDEZ PACED around her office and fumed. She billed more hours than any other associate in her law firm, she'd brought in new business, and yet her performance review stank! It was all about her lack of abilities as a team player, her condescending attitude. What in the world did that mean?

She needed to confront her boss, but she had absolutely no idea what to say.

The Ideal Performance Process

Believe it or not, under standard employment law, your employer has an obligation to treat you fairly. The basis for this standard is that employers must keep their promises with you, which was based on contract law. The courts have also implied parts of tort (personal injury) law into employee relationships. They have implied contracts between employees and companies and have implied sections of those contracts. Basically, the courts have said that every contract, including the basic employment contract, contains an implied covenant. A covenant is simply one section of a contract. That section requires the employer to treat you fairly. In employment law, this is called "the covenant of good faith and fair dealing."

Once you understand that every employee has a contract with your employer, it makes sense that they have to treat you fairly. In other kinds of contracts, the courts have said that if the parties to a contract are in an unequal bargaining position, the stronger party has an implied obligation to protect the weaker one.

In most jobs, the employees generally are the weaker parties. They have little say about the amount of pay they receive, the kind of work they do, and their working conditions.

> **"We need to talk"**
>
> Historically, courts held that if employees didn't like the working conditions, they could "vote with their feet" and leave. But in recent years, the courts have recognized that requiring employees to leave is unreasonable and creates too much hardship for them, especially for older employees. Over the years of looking at thousands of particular cases, the courts came to the conclusion that employers must treat employees fairly.

Fairness as the Standard

In an ideal world, all bosses would help employees achieve success by treating the employment relationship as an ongoing process of constant communication, dialogue, and specific and fair feedback. Managers would also give people positive comments and take the time to coach them to success.

Unfortunately, most bosses are far from ideal. The courts recognize this, so they have required managers to treat employees fairly only in specific situations, the most common of which is in evaluating performance.

> **"We need to talk"**
>
> Performance appraisals are key legal documents in every employment lawsuit. They are the official company documents, and so they should be done correctly.

Ideally, appraisals tell the story of the employee's life with the company. They should be given regularly—starting after three months and then at six months, and then yearly on the anniversary of the hire date.

When considering whether to take a case, lawyers on both sides will look at appraisals and ask whether the employee was a good performer for years who was then suddenly terminated. Obviously, this looks suspicious. But if the appraisals show a couple of years of declining performance, then a termination looks legitimate.

Sometimes appraisals show contradictory things such as years of substandard performance but continued pay increases. This might make a court conclude that the employer condoned the poor performance. It might be difficult for your boss to justify firing you then for poor performance. A court might ask—if you were performing so poorly—why they didn't just fire you?

A good appraisal should also compare this year to last year. If you've improved or deteriorated, the appraisal should say so. If the performance this year is significantly different than last year, it should say why.

If another boss wrote last year's appraisal, your boss now does have the right to rate you differently. They can also change your job responsibilities. Your boss must inform you of the new job requirements, either in the performance appraisals or other written memo, and you must be given time to achieve the new goals. As long as the assignments are achievable by a reasonable person, your boss can implement his or her desired changes, even if you can't achieve them.

Just the Facts, Please

Your boss has a responsibility to appraise your performance accurately. You would think this would be obvious, but it isn't. She needs to give specific, legitimate reasons for every criticism. Instead, many appraisals are conclusory. You're rated on attributes like attitude, leadership, and initiative. You can receive ratings on these qualities but she must give you facts to back up her conclusions in these categories.

Nobody is all good or all bad. Your boss, ideally, should find the good and praise it, but should also point out areas where you need to improve. If you've been rated "needs to improve" year after year, however, that looks suspicious. A court might say that your employer should have just terminated you instead.

If your company uses a numerical system, most people should come out in the middle—average—otherwise the system loses its meaning. Ideally, the form should give you an idea about how you did in certain categories, as well as the relative importance of those categories. For example, showing up on time is assumed for most jobs, so it should carry less weight than other items.

Some systems or managers like to have employees fill out the appraisals themselves to see what they think of their own performance, as well as to save time. This doesn't mean that your boss has to accept your self-assessment, but it does give you an opportunity to highlight your strengths, remind your boss of your wins, and cite specific examples. Give it your best shot.

Some bosses are also reluctant to fill out forms honestly because they don't like to criticize other people or they're afraid that they might make you mad. Many companies do not train managers sufficiently in how to do good reviews. You can turn this around to your advantage by filling out the form yourself, if they ask, or by e-mailing them a summary of your accomplishments for the year.

What Is a Bad Review?

Before we consider how to challenge a bad review, let's get some definitions. What is a bad review?

Well-known and well-regarded Denver psychiatrist Ron Rabin gives this advice to anyone seeking success in life—personal or professional:

"If there's one thing that I could tell someone that would most impact their success in life, it would be this: constantly ask for and listen to feedback—feedback at work, feedback about your relationship, feedback about life in general.

"I'm always trying to see if people are 'in sync' and get them back in sync if they're out of sync. The best way to get in sync is relentlessly seek feedback, listen, and then act on that feedback that's true and appropriate."

Or, as Mark Twain put it:

"Always acknowledge a fault. This will throw those in authority off their guard and give you an opportunity to commit more."

Depending on your outlook, a bad review can be anything from not getting an A+ to being put on probation. Many times employees think that they've had a bad performance review. However, this is not necessarily the case. It's not to say that there are never such things as bad reviews—clearly there are—but reviews can be too subjective, or too general to be useful. That said, they still hold some underlying truth.

The key is to honestly examine your own ability to listen to and absorb feedback. Is there any grain of truth in what your boss is saying? Anything you can learn from? At a minimum, you can always learn more about what your boss thinks of *you*. He or she may be dead wrong, crazy, or confused, but knowing what they think will always serve you. *Information is power.*

Playing the Cards You're Dealt

You may protest that your boss doesn't really see you. He or she doesn't really know you, or he or she may be an incompetent boss.

Any or all of those complaints may be legitimate but the sad truth is this: Your boss is your boss because someone above them thinks that they should be the boss. *That's it!* That is the most important reason. A failure to accept this existential truth leads to much employee misery.

Given that truth, how do you get the best out of your less-than-perfect boss, be they good, bad, or indifferent?

Here are my rules:

1. Look for what you can learn from them. Everyone excels at something. Perhaps the micromanager can teach you something about details—a skill you lack. A devilish boss can teach you about power—how and when to use it and when it's abused. A lazy boss can give you more responsibility and a chance to shine, as long as you're clever about making sure that you get credit for your own work.

2. Ask for feedback on a regular basis and listen for any grain of truth they impart.

3. Develop a relationship with your boss. The world runs on relationships. Everything you want at work you'll ultimately gain through relationships: promotions, pay increases, training opportunities, travel—whatever rocks your world. Of course, you have to be good at what you do, but, usually, those who succeed have some competitive combination of work and relationship skills. So, no matter what you like to do, learning relationship skills is a must.

4. Ask for details. The devil is in the details and you have to get them. Most performance reviews that I would call "bad" are simply not detailed enough with specific examples. Instead, they rest on generalities in a way that doesn't serve the employee because it's not behaviorally specific.

5. Depersonalize the issue. Take the time to step back and try not to take it personally. More about this rule later in the chapter.

6. Document your conversation. After your talk with your boss, e-mail or write a note to her confirming what you talked about. This helps bolster your case for the next performance review or raise request if you've followed through on what you said you'd change in response to her critique. It will allow you a documentation leg up on your next performance review and/or request for a new status.

How to Ask for Specifics

The key then, in challenging a bad review, is to ask for specifics. Why specifics? Both employment law and general principles of good management require managers to give specific examples and to be behaviorally specific, meaning that they need to tell you what you *said or did wrong* and *what you need to do or say differently to improve*. If it's not something that you can say or do, it's not behaviorally specific enough.

The following chart illustrates this point.

Vague	Behaviorally specific
You have a bad attitude.	You yelled at one customer and came in late.
You're lousy at Outlook.	You need to improve your scheduling skills by taking a class in Outlook.
Your work is careless.	You made three spelling errors in a letter that went to a client and you neglected to proof several quarterly reports.

If you find that you have comments that fall more into the first column than the second one, learn to challenge that by asking for behavioral specifics, using the 1-2-3 Go! format from Chapter 1.

For example, an administrative clerk sued Air France for discrimination. Specifically, she claimed that her performance review indicated that she was being treated differently because of her gender. The comments included things such as "she was too emotional," with no specific examples.

She won her case because such statements were found to be examples of gender stereotypes and evidence of sex discrimination.

My client Karen, for example, whose frustration with her review (described in the opening of this chapter), received a document from her boss laced with comments such as "not a team player" and "condescending attitude," with no specific examples or explanations as to what those terms mean. I coached Karen to ask for specific examples that helped her understand and improve.

Timing Is Everything

Many employers now have a system where they hand out performance reviews before you meet with your boss. This can be useful since you then have time to absorb and think about what questions you have (not to mention, compose yourself so that you don't scream or get out of hand when you talk with your boss).

If you don't have such a system, I do not advise you do this in the first meeting where you receive your performance review. Wait until you've had time to digest the feedback and then return.

Read the review, think about it, and try to *depersonalize* the issue.

What does this mean? Let's say, for example, that you have a lazy or uneducated boss who writes comments such as the general ones above. Rather than taking on the idea that *you* are careless, you need to rewrite the review in your own mind so that it's the *mistakes* that are examples of carelessness. It's never good for your own sense of yourself to take on a critical review as your whole personality.

There's no question that negative feedback hurts. It's the rare person who can just shrug it off, but it's useful to put it in perspective. Most of us, when we're stopped by the state patrol for flying down the highway, do not leap out of our car and exclaim: "Thank you for stopping me sir! I'm so glad you did! Please write me a ticket immediately! I could have hurt someone!"

Your weaknesses are not who you are. We all have strengths and weaknesses. A weakness is simply an example of where you need to improve; it's not you. Identifying a weakness will help you to:

- Understand where you need to focus your efforts
- Realize that you have failed to communicate with your boss
- See if your boss is just plain, flat-out wrong
- Decide if you're in the wrong job

The first step is to separate who you are from the process of letting you know where you need to improve.

After you've had time to review the feedback, write out a list of specific questions. It can also be helpful to practice the conversation with a friend. You role-play your boss, anticipating what questions he might ask, while your friend plays you, simply asking the questions you've written out. If you can anticipate your boss's reactions, it will help you feel more prepared and relaxed when you actually have the conversation. It can also help you see where you need to get to know your boss better. If you find that you have trouble anticipating your boss's responses, you need to develop more of a relationship. Remember the rule from the last chapter: there's no rule that says you can't ask your boss to lunch.

Getting to Know You
When you struggle with difficult people, it is almost always caused by a failure of relationship. We don't take enough time to

build the relationships that we need to build that will help us be successful.

Chief Justice Earl Warren, for example, wanted to make sure that he had agreement about the historic school segregation case of *Brown vs. Board of Education.* He knew that would be an enormous struggle. He started, over a period of months, taking the separate justices to lunch to help build a consensus. He took one justice to lunch twenty times before they developed an agreement.

How many times have you taken your problem boss to lunch? Twenty? Twice? Zero? In some way, you need to take the time to develop that relationship. Ideally, of course, your boss should take the initiative and do this for you, but some bosses lack relationship skills also.

After you meet with your boss, document what you both said and send her an e-mail or written memo summarizing your conversation. Be sure to ask her to let you know if there's anything in the confirmation that's different from what she remembers or anything additional that she thinks you should do to correct the problem. If she does come up with something, be sure to respond in writing, or better yet, in person, in order to make sure that you're both on the same page in terms of what you need to do to improve.

Appealing to a Higher Authority

If you've taken all the steps in this chapter to challenge your performance review and still don't feel satisfied with her answer, you'll need to consider appealing to a higher authority: your boss's boss, HR, or your organization's head.

Think long and hard before you take this step. The truth is none of us likes criticism, and your boss is no exception. We especially don't like to hear it delivered from someone else—what I call triangulation—instead of from the person who thinks that we need to shape up.

Try, try, and try again to fix your relationship with your boss before you appeal his decision.

When you do decide to go to his boss or HR, be sure that you've documented all of your conversations, and e-mailed confirming summaries of those conversations to your boss, as outlined earlier. This will impress whatever higher authorities you appeal to because they will know that you've done your very best to sort things out directly.

When you do complain to this authority—about your bad performance review or anything else—be sure that you've documented facts, not just your conclusions, assumptions, or biases. It's a fact that your boss wrote that you "had a bad attitude." It's an assumption that he did so because someone else spread an untrue rumor about you. It's a fact that he didn't give you any specific examples of what you can do to change this review. It's a conclusion that he did so because he suffers from an attitude problem himself!

Taking a calm and unemotional approach, detailing the facts, and offering up your documentation will serve you best with any higher authority. Be sure that you mention that you appreciate the difficult position you may be putting this person in by going to them instead of your boss, but don't be apologetic. You have a right to a detailed, factual, and useful performance review. Your boss is not doing his or her job if they can't give you what you've earned.

Sample Script

MARY: Mr. Lazy Boss, may I speak with you about my performance review?

MR. LAZY: I guess so, but I thought we already talked about it.

MARY: Yes, but now that I've had time to think about it, I realized that I have some additional questions. I know how busy you are and I understand that you may only have allowed a certain amount of time for reviews, but I would really like to spend about fifteen minutes with you finding out what you think about some specific questions. (Step 1: Offers understanding and appreciation.)

MR. LAZY: Okay, shoot.

MARY: To start, I see that you've written that I'm careless. Could you give me a couple of examples of what you mean so that I can improve on that core issue?

MR. LAZY: Well that's obvious, isn't it? I mean you're just not careful enough.

MARY: (Exhibiting persistence.) I appreciate that you think that but I need to understand more specifically what you mean so that I can improve. Could you give me an example?

MR. LAZY: Well, the Roberts report. It went out with all kinds of typos in it.

MARY: Hmmm. I see. (Mary knows that Mr. Lazy was the last person to work on that draft but she refrains, at this point, from saying that to Mr. Lazy. Timing is everything.) It's helpful to know what you think. Do you have any other examples?

MR. LAZY: I'm always getting complaints from clients that they can't find their records. I know that I tell you to send them copies every quarter.

MARY: (Pretty sure that she's never been told any such thing but refrains from mentioning this.) So, what I'm hearing is that in the future we need to have a system whereby reports go out every quarter to clients and we make sure there are no typos in them, is that correct?

MR. LAZY: Yes, I think that's it.

MARY: I'm just wondering how I can make sure that this happens in every case. For the Roberts report, for example, I didn't see the final copy of the report before it went out. I'm wondering if we could have a system where you could send me the final after you're finished with it so that I can make sure there are no typos in it before it goes out. Would that work for you?

MR. LAZY: Sure.

MARY: And I'm now very clear that you want all clients to receive copies of their record every quarter. I didn't understand that before.

MR. LAZY: Oh, well . . .

MARY: Is there anything else that would help my work be better and deal with your concern about these careless mistakes? (Depersonalizes the issue by not talking about "herself" as being careless, but as the "mistakes" as being careless.)

MR. LAZY: No, not that I can think of.

MARY: Well, I really appreciate your having this conversation with me. I know how busy you are. (Closes with understanding and appreciation.) What I'd like to do is shoot you an e-mail with my understanding of what we've agreed upon. (Document everything.) I really want to do the best possible job for you every day. (Closes on a positive note.)

MR. LAZY: No problem.

In the situation with Karen, who opened this chapter, she tried to talk with her boss but failed to make any progress. She was forced to appeal to a higher authority.

Sample Script

KAREN: Ms. Higher Authority, I need to talk to you about my performance review. I'm concerned because I've tried to work it out with my boss but he doesn't seem to be able to help me with my concerns.

MS. H.A.: Okay, what seems to be the problem?

KAREN: I understand that it's my responsibility as an employee here to try to work things out directly with my boss (Offers understanding.), and I really have tried to do exactly that. I've had five conversations with him over the past month and tried to summarize what I thought we both said afterwards so there would be no misunderstanding. Here are printouts of my e-mails.

MS. H.A.: Hmm. How did this all start?

KAREN: It was over my performance review. It included comments such as I was "not a team player" and that I had a "condescending attitude." I realize that he thought he was explaining things by writing those comments but I needed more detail in order to be able to change my behavior. I've had all these meetings with him but I'm still not getting what I need.

MS. H.A.: What specifically do you want me to do?

KAREN: What I need is for you to look at these and then perhaps you could coach my manager into putting it into something more specific. If I had details on what I did wrong and how I could improve, I think that I could give him what he wants. I love my job and want to be able to do my very best for the organization.

MS. H.A.: Let me take a look at them and I'll call you back.

KAREN: Great. I know how busy you are and I really appreciate your help.

Boss Communication Don'ts	Boss Communication Dos
Disregard a bad review.	Look for what you personally can learn from negative feedback.
Accept generalities.	Ask for specific details.
Fail to document.	Confirm conversations with e-mail or memos.
Give up.	Keep talking and writing.
Accept an incompetent boss's final word.	Appeal to a higher authority.

Chapter 3

How to Ask for a Raise, Promotion, or Other Benefits

LARRY PETERSON STARTED to pour himself a third cup of coffee and then stopped. He was jittery enough, he decided. He needed a raise but knew that his boss's skinflint attitude wouldn't provide a good chance. But his wife, Mary, was pregnant with their third child, their credit cards had maxed out, and their adjustable rate mortgage was ready to adjust them out of their house. He knew he deserved a raise because he put more hours in than anyone else and consistently came up with new ideas to improve their systems. He'd promised Mary that he'd talk to his boss today but he had absolutely, positively no idea what to say.

What to Say and What Not to Say: More Money

Most employees launch their plea for more money with the same theme: I *need* more money! I have kids, a house, car payments, school debts, or whatever. Big mistake.

The focus needs to be not on what you *need* but on what you can contribute to the organization. Let's start here:

- Make a list of all your accomplishments since your last raise.
- Survey your clients or customers, if they have a close relationship with you, for what they think you contribute to their service.
- Talk with coworkers or other managers about how you've helped them. If possible, find some of these people to write letters for you.
- Find out the market rate for your kind of job in your industry, and for your size of organization.
- Do your homework. If possible, find out what others in your organization are making.

Many companies discourage or outright forbid employees from talking about salaries. It's my opinion—and the opinion of many other employment attorneys—that to do so is a violation of the National Labor Relations Act (NLRA), which allows employees the power to organize, even if they're not trying to form a union. Discussing salaries, raises, or benefits is a type of organizing activity, and you have the right to organize. What is one of the main things that employees want to organize about? Salary, of course, which is hard to discuss if you don't know what others are making.

Discrimination in Raises or Promotions
If you find out that others are making more than you or are being promoted without merit, you may want to dig deeper into your options. Obviously, it's illegal to pay or promote someone differently because of their race, gender, age or other protected characteristic, and you may think those sorts of obvious claims had disappeared but unfortunately, that's not true.

Promotions need to be based on objective criteria in order to avoid discrimination—and this is another area where employers frequently fail to meet the legal requirements.

Discrimination may not be obvious. Race or gender discrimination cases today frequently reflect subtle forms of bias. If an employer has no objective criteria for deciding promotions or raises, for example, that may lead to decisions based on subtle forms of discrimination.

For example, consider the case decided by the U.S. Supreme Court in 1988. Clara Watson, who is black, was hired by a bank in 1973. After three years, she was promoted to drive-in teller. Four years later, she applied for the job of supervisor of lobby tellers. A white male was promoted instead. Then she applied for supervisor of drive-in tellers, but a white female got the job.

For the next year, Ms. Watson worked informally as the assistant to the new supervisor of lobby tellers. When he left, she applied for his job. It was given to the woman who had been drive-in teller supervisor.

She applied for the drive-in supervisor job. It was given to another white male. She sued for race discrimination.

The U.S. Supreme Court ruled in her favor. The court noted the company did not have any precise or formal criteria to back up these decisions. Instead, the managers relied on their subjective judgment of who would do a better job. This is not only illegal but also doesn't make much business sense.

Find out if you're being treated differently because of some protected characteristic—age, sex, race, pregnancy, and so on. If so, you should ask to be treated the same as others when it comes to raises and promotions. If you're denied advancement because of one of these issues, see Chapter 4 about how to complain about discrimination.

Making Your Case for Raises, Promotions, or Other Opportunities

First, do not rely on opinions, conclusions, or assumptions. Document the facts. Notice the difference:

Conclusion or assumption	Fact
I am a good salesperson.	I had over $1 million in sales last year.
I am a hard worker.	I arrive every morning at 7 A.M. and leave at 6 P.M.
I am good at customer service.	Three clients have written letters praising my customer service efforts.

See the difference? You'll have to build your case just as you would a case in court, with facts, examples, and testimony—not opinions, conclusions, or rumors.

If you have any kind of job where you can quantify your contribution with numbers, that's clearly the best way to let your boss understand your contribution: hours worked or billed, sales made, customer service letters or awards.

If your work is more subjective, you can still build your portfolio by using some of the suggestions above, such as interviews with other managers, clients, or coworkers.

Build your case first; then talk. When you do talk with your boss, you'll probably end up needing to negotiate.

Negotiation Basics

Good negotiation is all about *why*: why do you want what you want, and why do they want what they want? My own technique is classic interest-based negotiation; it's all about finding out what the underlying reason is why someone wants or does not want something, instead of buying into whatever their superficial reason might be.

Take the classic raise situation: you want a raise; your boss doesn't want to give you a raise. Stalemate, right?

Only if you neglect to answer one question: why?

Consider, for example, the classic negotiation story of two sisters and an orange. The two sisters are living in a remote location—far from any convenience store—and they both want the one orange they have in the house. They're stuck in a classic struggle: "I want the orange." "No, I want the orange." "No, I want the orange," and on and on. But the underlying "*why*" is not answered in this, or in most negotiations.

So then the question becomes: why might someone want an orange? Perhaps to use the zest for cooking, the juice for making the cake, or (if he or she is a Martha Stewart devotee), to stick cloves in it and hang it in a closet. If the two sisters are stuck in their *positions* (the statements that they both want the orange), rather than their *interests* (the reason *why* they want the orange), little progress can be made. But if they're both willing to answer why they want it and reveal their underlying interest, they may both be able to get what they want.

With raises, for example, it's important to discover not just that your boss has a position of not giving raises this year, but the underlying reasons why. He may opine that there is no money in the budget for raises, but perhaps there's money in someone else's budget that can be shifted to your department, or perhaps you can have a phased raise, some this year and some the next.

And why else might your manager not want to give you a raise? Perhaps because he's afraid that if he gives you one, you'll blab, and then he'll have to give everyone else more money. Perhaps he doesn't realize that you'd be willing to work longer hours and/or make more sales to make up the difference.

Consider yourself a detective: ferret out his reasons and delve deeper into the whys. When you're talking to your boss, keep asking, in a respectful way, *why* he thinks as he does. Ask him to explain his answers. Ask what other solutions he's considered to whatever problem he's raised. Ask when he first started thinking this way. If you keep asking questions, you'll eventually uncover his reasoning. When you do, you'll then be able to know how to proceed to suggest alternatives to meeting his objectives.

As mentioned earlier, your whys should not be revealed as your needs, as in "I need a raise." But you can and should reveal why you deserve a raise.

Finding Common Ground

You want to try to find common ground. What this means is that you need to find a way to frame both the problem and the solution in a way that meets both your needs and those of your boss.

Attaining a Promotion

Promotions are increasingly difficult to gain in many organizations these days. Why? Because many organizations are loaded at the top with baby boomers who are waiting longer to retire for financial reasons, creating bottlenecks that are challenging to crash through. A promotion may not be in the cards for you for reasons that are far from your boss's fault.

If this is the problem in your organization, you may be able to meet your needs for recognition by taking on different kinds of work or jobs or by seeking a lateral transfer to a different department. This may meet your needs for more intellectual or social stimulation, even if it doesn't come with the title you'd like.

Receiving Other Benefits

Instead of a promotion, you may also want to negotiate hard for growth or training opportunities. Learning new skills may be worth more to you in the long run than the promotion or raise. Ask to join a team that will teach you how to do something new. Request a spot working with the clients on the most innovative projects. Ask for a training budget and attend new seminars.

You might also ask for a mentor instead of a promotion, if you find a promotion is impossible. Go to HR and ask them—they've been doing this for a long time and should be able to find a good match. A mentor can serve you through this job and the rest of your career if you work on cultivating that relationship.

If your boss indicates that you've earned a promotion but she doesn't have the budget or authority, request flextime or work-at-home options instead. Perhaps you can negotiate one or two days at home, if they're not willing to go the distance for an entire work-at-home schedule.

All these options might be worth even more to you in the long run than a regular promotion or raise.

You may also have to negotiate hard about training situations. Perhaps the budget is limited this year for conferences in Vail or Maui, but a local course or an online training program might be within the budget. Don't get fixed on only one solution to your training needs. Try to come armed with several different solutions—even if you have one in particular that you'd love to have come through. You might even, for example, suggest that you pay the travel expenses or use your frequent flyer miles if the company will pay the costs of the training itself.

It Never Hurts to Ask

When I used to teach law students, I always drilled into them that the one rule of practicing law was: *"It never hurts to ask!"*

What is the answer to these questions, I would ask: *Can we do the contract differently? Can I have more time to write this brief? Can we work out a settlement to this dispute? Can you pay my client more money?*

It never hurts to ask! was always a correct answer in my class. Sometimes you have to ask a question several times, or you just have to keep being persistent until you get what you deserve!

Of course, you want to do this in a charming and diplomatic way so that it doesn't become harassment, but persistence does pay off. In most situations you have nothing to lose by asking.

One of my clients, for example, longed to move from her challenging HR position into internal consulting, but the company had no such position. After coaching from me that involved digging out what she really wanted as well as role-playing possible solutions, she marshaled her courage to present a proposal to her boss and was discouraged when it was turned down. I looked over her proposition and made several suggestions such as including more details about how the position would be structured, and she took the reformatted proposal back to her boss several months later.

That time, he bit. She's now happily focusing on serving as an internal consultant to groups needing her skills as an arbitrator, instead of dealing with the HR processes she had come to loathe.

In most situations, you have nothing to lose by asking. Even if the answer is no, learn to ask for something else instead. Many times your boss will feel guilty enough that he's said no about whatever you just asked that he will be open to giving you some other perk instead.

When you go in to ask for that promotion, for example, come armed with several other things, as suggested in this section, that you might want as fallback requests. Then, in the event your boss turns you down, you're ready with the next pitch. Sooner or later he or she will say yes, just to get you out the door!

"We need to talk"

All of this, of course, requires you to hold your nerves steady in order to withstand the stress of conflict and negotiation—something that's difficult for many people. Most people think of conflict as something to avoid at all costs. This kind of challenging conversation requires you to see conflict as transformative, something that I wrote about in my book *The Power of a Good Fight*.

Transform Conflict

Most people view conflict as a sign of dysfunction and something to be avoided. If you can embrace conflict as something that can lead to more creativity and innovation, you will be ahead of the game. How do you transform conflict? In my experience as a litigator, mediator, and consultant, it takes three things: attitude, skills, and purpose.

You have to change your attitude about conflict. Instead of seeing conflict as a problem to be avoided, try seeing it as an opportunity to develop a more creative solution to whatever problem you're facing than you would have had if you'd avoided the subject. While staying in a constructive dialogue and working your way through conflict is never easy, the outcome can bring surprising and beneficial results that would never have been possible without conflict.

You must build key skills. While most people think that they can learn how to use a computer, master a recipe, or read directions on MapQuest, they may not think of mastering conflict as a skill. Conflict, by my definition, is just a negotiation that we don't know we're having. Once we decide to negotiate during the conflict, it's just a matter of improving our negotiation skills. Books, seminars and websites on conflict and negotiation abound (including mine!); take advantage of these resources to improve your skills.

You need to have a purpose in order to master conflict. Working your way through difficult workplace discussions that create—or have the potential to create—conflict is challenging and can be draining. But having a higher purpose to our work and life to focus on during the discussion will fuel our drive to succeed. If we don't have a higher purpose, such discussions can be excruciating to muddle through.

So when you're in the midst of asking for a raise, a promotion, or any other challenging request, keep your eye on the prize, and remember that it's just a matter of the three keys: attitude, skills, and purpose.

Sample Script

LARRY: Mr. Stingy, I need to talk with you. Would now be a good time?

MR. STINGY: Okay.

LARRY: I'd like to review my progress at the firm. I'm proud of what I've been able to accomplish on XYZ project and I know that the clients are also. I've brought a copy of the letter they wrote to Mr. Senior Manager. I also have billable hours this year that average 200 per month. My current compensation seems to be lagging both behind the market (Used specifics; did homework—most bosses know that they need to be within the market in order to keep good employees, not at the top of the market but somewhere within striking distance.) as well as behind what I think that I contribute to the firm. I'd like you to consider raising me by 20 percent.

MR. STINGY: Really? I had no idea we were that far behind. Let me look at those numbers and talk to HR. Hmmm. HR might be a problem.

LARRY: Why is that?

MR. STINGY: Well, they like to have everyone at the same grade level and so they may rebel against raising you up at a different rate than others in your same job classification.

LARRY: I thought of that. (Did homework.) But if we raised me up to a mid-band level and changed my title to customer focus instead of customer service, it might work. Plus, I'd be more than willing to stay late and take over some of the closing paperwork you do.

MR. STINGY: Wow! Now, that's an attractive offer. You know how I hate that kind of paperwork. Let me get back to you tomorrow.

Boss Communication Don'ts	Boss Communication Dos
Talk about needs.	Talk about contribution.
Go in unprepared.	Do your homework.
Take whatever answer you're given.	Learn to negotiate.
Allow discrimination.	Learn the law.
Be afraid to ask.	Ask.

Chapter 4

How to Complain about Harassment, Discrimination, Threats, Violence, or Unsafe Conditions

CARLA KING FUMED as she stripped off her clunky fireman's suit. All her attempts to break into the "boys' club" of her small-town fire department had been for naught. Her training instructor had just slammed her again for hose layout and scuba violations. He critiqued her every move. None of the guys in training had to put up with that kind of scrutiny. She was ready to march into the chief's office right now! The only problem was she had absolutely, positively no idea what to say.

Understanding Harassment

The first step is to understand your legal rights. I'll cover some of the more common complaints in this section. Be aware, however, that some federal laws on these issues do not apply if you work for an employer with fewer than fifteen (in some cases) or fifty (in other situations) employees. Also, government employees are frequently subject to different rules, and union contracts may provide additional wrinkles. In this chapter I offer a general educational overview of the problem. As always, you need to research the laws and policies that govern your particular state and employer, and you may need to consult an attorney.

Illegal Harassment and Discrimination: True Legal Violations

The term "illegal harassment" implies that there's such a thing as legal harassment, and in fact, there is. Harassment and discrimination claims remain the most common legal complaints in the workplace, but what constitutes illegal harassment and discrimination seems to be the subject of endless workplace confusion.

This is because the law sets a floor for workplace behavior. Let's call it the "red zone." Many organizations have a policy that is stricter than the law requires. Furthermore, every court in the country has held that companies may have a stricter policy and can discipline people who violate that policy even if the behavior in no way violates the law. Behavior that merely "offends" someone, however, is not a legal problem. There are different standards that must be met before it qualifies as such.

Harassment and Discrimination Legal Standards

Federal laws prohibit discrimination, harassment, and retaliation based on "protected characteristics" such as the following:

- Sex or gender
- Age (age discrimination against those 40 and older)
- Race and color
- Religion
- National origin
- Citizenship
- Physical disability (this may include emotional or mental disabilities)
- Pregnancy
- Veteran/military status
- Family and medical leave

Harassment because of sex includes:

- Sexual harassment
- Gender harassment
- Same-sex harassment
- Harassment based on pregnancy

If you live in California you have some additional protection. California has perhaps the strictest laws in the country on these issues and also prohibits discrimination, harassment, and retaliation because of:

- Status as a domestic violence victim
- Medical condition or genetic characteristic
- Ancestry
- Marital status

- Sexual orientation
- Childbirth and related medical conditions

Many people are confused about the difference between harassment, discrimination, and retaliation. Harassment is not, in fact, based on a new law but something that has been around since the 1964 Civil Rights Act. It is one kind of discrimination.

The first U.S. Supreme Court case to consider the issue involved a bank teller who had sex with a bank officer for years. She argued in court that she felt coerced to have a relationship with her boss in order to keep her job. The Supreme Court agreed that her claim could be illegal sexual harassment.

Discrimination is an adverse job action taken by a supervisor because of the individual's protected characteristics (as listed earlier). Adverse job actions include failure to hire or promote, firing or a layoff, cuts in pay, a denial of salary increase, and changing other terms or conditions of employment such as hours or vacation time because of a protected characteristic.

Retaliation is an action taken against someone for protesting, complaining, or cooperating in the investigation of discrimination or harassment. This action can include any adverse job action or physical retaliation such as physical threats, assault or battery, destruction of personal property, or stalking.

Quid Pro Quo Harassment

Harassment can be an adverse job action or physical, visual, or verbal action. In the "red zone," there is true illegal harassment, known as *quid pro quo* ("this for that"). This takes the form of "you have to date me to get this job" or "you have to have sex with me to get this promotion." This type of harassment usually involves a colleague or superior leveraging job favors for sexual favors. The harasser is someone who actually has the power to grant such favors, either by express or implied threats. Quid pro quo can also be implied by repeated propositions. As the harassee, you must, however, show that the harassment had some impact on your job such as you were denied an annual pay increase, laid off, or forced to quit.

SEXUAL FAVORITISM
Another type of illegal harassment is illegal sexual favoritism. If the situation involves isolated instances of management giving favorable treatment to paramours, then in most cases, it isn't illegal, although it probably violates your organization's policy. It is illegal if sexual favoritism is widespread in the company.

HOSTILE ENVIRONMENT
An "illegal hostile environment" is an accusation that many people hurl around carelessly to describe their workplace. Many people seem to think that they are in a hostile environment if someone's behavior offends them. Not true. In order to prove a true hostile environment you have to show the existence of the following four key factors:

1. The behavior was discriminating or sexually harassing in tone and nature. This means that it was based on one of the protected characteristics above, meaning not just that someone is harassing you, but that they are harassing you specifically because of your sex, race, color, or religion, and so on.

Contrary to popular belief, in most states there's no such thing as illegal "general" harassment. If it's not tied to one of these protected classifications, it is not illegal. However, general harassment may violate criminal laws (assault, stalking, threats, etc.) if it is severe enough.

2. You must prove that the behavior is unwelcome by the victim, meaning that you didn't encourage the behavior or participate in it.
3. In order to prove illegal harassment, you must show that it was severe, meaning that it interfered with work.
4. You have to prove that the employer knew, or should have known, about the harassment and did nothing.

You must be able to prove all four of these factors in order to prove illegal harassment under the law.

ILLEGAL RETALIATION

Illegal retaliation is another type of harassment. In this action, you are retaliated against by a supervisor, peer, subordinate, or outsider for refusing sexual advances, for complaining about harassment or discrimination, or for assisting in a claim. This retaliation can take many forms, such as demotion, poor performance appraisals, bad job assignments, termination, threats, or violence.

For example, I was once asked to conduct an investigation on a retaliation claim involving an employee at a high-tech company.

He alleged that he was retaliated against because he had testified as a witness in a racial discrimination case. He claimed that the VP involved in the case "belittled" him in meetings after he testified. While this might have been a good claim of retaliation, my investigation revealed that this particular VP treated other employees exactly the same way and that the employee himself had been treated in the same manner *before* the lawsuit.

Harassment or Discrimination under Your Organization's Policies

Employers can, and frequently do, prohibit all harassment under their own policies, not just harassment based on race, sex, or other protected characteristics. This may include all behavior that is disrespectful. Check your organization's policies, which should be posted in the workplace or on the website. You may be surprised to learn how broad it is. A typical statement might look like this:

Workplace Harassment

*   *   *

ABC Company is committed to providing all employees with a work environment free from hostility and harassment and provides this policy to express that commitment. We recognize that harassment of employees in any form destroys morale, impairs productivity, and is not permissible in a productive, cooperative environment.

*   *   *

ABC Company will carefully investigate and vigorously enforce all reported violations of this policy. Harassment by management or coworkers including but not limited to harassment based upon race, sex, color, religion, national origin, age, disability, or veteran status, whether verbally or physically, will not be tolerated. Harassing language or actions are not only a violation of company policy, but may constitute an illegal act. We will comply with all federal, state, and/or local laws.

* * *

ABC Company prohibits workplace harassment of every kind, including sexually related conduct of a physical, verbal, or visual nature that creates an intimidating, hostile, seductive, or offensive work environment; unwanted touching, patting, grabbing, repeated objectionable sexual flirtations, propositions, suggestive comments, lewd jokes, and display in the workplace of sexually explicit objects, drawings, or photos. Of course, ABC Company also prohibits any employee from making unwelcome sexual advances or requests for sexual favors when submission or rejection of such conduct is used as the basis for employment-related decisions.

* * *

Statements that say the employer prohibits harassment "in any form" have become quite common in most workplaces. These statements can provide you with powerful ammunition when you confront the person whose boorish behavior may be borderline harassment and/or when you need to talk to your manager or HR.

Examples of Legal or Policy Violations
If you're still confused about what really crosses the line into legal or policy violations, check out the following list from one of our clients:

- Objectionable comments about a person's age, race, skin color, national origin, ethnic background, religion, gender, marital status, disability or medical problem, age, or veteran status
- Repeated and unwelcome requests for a date
- Racial, sexual orientation, sexist, age-related or sexual jokes or comments
- Referring to a coworker in demeaning language ("babe," "girl"/"boy," "broad," "colored," "cripple," "grandpa"/"grandma," "pops")
- Following a person inside or outside of work
- Making sexual gestures
- Wearing or displaying the Confederate flag
- Accessing or displaying sexual or racial pictures, cartoons, or websites
- Unwelcoming touching of a person's hair, clothing, or body
- Unwelcome kissing, hugging, or patting
- Wearing or displaying hate-related symbols (such as a swastika)
- Restraining or blocking the path of a person
- Touching oneself in a way that is suggestive in view of a coworker
- Spreading rumors about a coworker's sex life, including affairs, marital status, or sexual orientation
- Repeatedly leering at a coworker
- Making sexually suggestive facial expressions (winking, blowing kisses)
- Treating someone differently after a legally protected medical or family leave
- Neglecting to consider a woman with small children for a job that requires travel

- Refusing to consider an older applicant because he or she is "overqualified"

Note: The preceding list of examples does not include all potential legal or policy violations.

There is always a question, of course, of whether your organization is willing to enforce the law and its policies. There is also the personal issue of whether you want to raise this with anyone for fear of formal or informal retaliation. We'll deal more fully with those issues in later chapters.

Values Violations

In addition to formal policy statements, many organizations also have values statements. While these may seem as familiar and useless as wallpaper, you would be well advised to check them out, read them, and ponder whether any of the behavior you're receiving at work seems to violate the organization's stated values. These values may include things such as "people are our most important resource," "we respect all our employees," and so on.

Although it's easy to become cynical about whether the organization really stands behind and intends to enforce these messages, if you bring them up at the appropriate time (more about this in later chapters), such as when you're talking to the person engaging in the problem behavior or your manager or HR, it can be an incredibly skillful move. What I'm suggesting here is something along the lines of "Ed is doing X. When I was thinking about X, I started wondering if X was consistent with our values as a company. In looking at our statement of values in our policy manual, I see that we say Y. It just doesn't seem to me that Ed's behavior is consistent with our company values. Could you please clarify for me what is acceptable under our values statements?"

Other Workplace Legal Issues

Other examples of clearly illegal behavior in the workplace include issues such as your supervisor denying you legitimate breaks or overtime if you're an hourly worker, failing to allow you appropriate time off under the Family and Medical Leave Act (FMLA), engaging in disability discrimination and/or failing to allow appropriate accommodations if you have a disability, or denying workers' compensation, whistle-blower protection, or privacy.

Hourly Versus Exempt Qualifications

In order to establish if you are in fact entitled to overtime, you must first know whether or not you are an exempt or hourly employee. If you are exempt, what exactly are you exempt from? Being paid overtime. If you do not have significant supervisory responsibilities and/or high-level administrative or technical expertise, you're hourly. Many employers wrongly characterize someone as "salary" in order to avoid overtime. This is illegal unless you meet the legal definition of exempt. If you're non-exempt, you have a right to be paid overtime.

Failure to Allow Family and Medical Leave

You have a right to twelve weeks a year of unpaid leave after your first year of employment to take care of a serious health condition for you or an immediate family member. Being denied this is illegal under the Family and Medical Leave Act (FMLA). You do not need to take this time off all at once but can do it in increments, as long as the total is no more than twelve weeks per year.

Disability

You have a right to be accommodated if you have a disability and your employer can reasonably accommodate you without undue hardship. Accommodations may include a special screen for your computer, a special chair because of back problems, or a flexible schedule to accommodate doctor's appointments. Time off may also be appropriate. You may not be denied a promotion or job because of a disability if you are able to do the work with a reasonable accommodation.

Whistle-blower Protection

You can't be fired or disciplined for reporting a violation of the law or for refusing to violate a law. One of the first whistle-blower cases involved a man who was called to testify against his employer in an IRS case. His boss came in the day before he was scheduled to testify and said he should lie when he testified in court the next day because if he told the truth they would lose. The employee said that he couldn't lie because he would be under oath. The boss replied that he could do what he liked but "I'm just telling you: tell the truth and you'll be fired!"

Sure enough, the employee told the truth and they canned him. When he sued, the court ruled that it was the public policy of the state of California (and every other state) for people to tell the truth in court and an employee can't be fired for doing so. This became known as the whistle-blower protection, and several different federal statutes, in addition to court cases, protect your right to complain about legal or public policy violations in the workplace, as well as to refuse to violate the law.

You have a right to work in a safe environment. At the federal level, the Occupational Health and Safety Administration (OSHA) governs safe working environments. You have a right to complain if your company is violating OSHA standards. Moreover, if you complain to OSHA that your employer has ignored your complaints to them, you are protected under the whistle-blower protection described in this section.

Wrongful Termination and Other Wrongful Actions

Believe it or not, the law implies that in employment relationships, you have a right to be treated fairly, as long as you are performing your duties and responsibilities as an employee in a reasonable way. This has been interpreted to mean that you should be warned before you're fired; be given the promotions you were promised; and generally be treated with "good faith and fair dealings."

The Consumer Product Safety Commission governs the safety of consumer goods. If you are aware that your company is making unsafe goods, you have a right to complain. If the company does not respond, you are protected under the whistle-blower protection laws explained in this section.

One of the first such cases in the country was a case brought by a gentleman named Mr. Pugh against See's Candy Company. Mr. Pugh started out working on the line making candy. Over the course of his thirty-two-year career, he worked his way up to vice president.

Over time, Mr. Pugh and the president of the company became friends; they and their spouses even traveled and socialized together. The four had just returned from a golfing vacation in Spain. The day after the trip, Mr. Pugh walked into the president's office, and the president abruptly fired him. When Mr. Pugh asked why, the president simply responded "Look deep within your heart and you will find the answer." No other explanation was offered. Mr. Pugh looked deep within his heart, found the name of an attorney, and sued! He won the case. The court said that it was a violation of the "covenant of good faith and fair dealing" to fire a long-term employee with no warning.

Disability

If you have a "permanent impairment of a major life function," your employer must put you on disability coverage. What is a "major life function"? Generally, things such as working, eating, sleeping, and walking are considered major life functions.

Privacy Violations

In most states, you have a right to keep your private life private at work. Inappropriate or unwelcome questions about your personal life, medical issues, or after-work activities could violate your privacy.

You have a right, for example, to march in a KKK parade or a gay rights rally on your non-work time. Even if your employer finds out about these activities and disapproves, in most states, you cannot be fired, disciplined, or harassed because of these non-work-time pursuits.

How to Handle Threats and Violence

You have a right to be safe at work. If someone's threatening physical harm or engaging in physical abuse at work, he's violating the law, as well as, most likely, your employer's policy. Most organizations have strong statements against threats and violence similar to this one:

* * *

All employees have a strong interest in and responsibility for helping to maintain a safe working environment for themselves and their coworkers. The company strives to ensure a safe environment for all employees, and this policy is issued and administered to support this commitment.

* * *

The company and its employees will have zero tolerance for threats and violent acts in the workplace. Examples of this could include intimidating, threatening, or hostile behaviors such as physical abuse, vandalism, arson, sabotage, use of weapons, carrying weapons onto company property, or any other act which in management's opinion is inappropriate to the workplace.

* * *

Employees who observe or have knowledge of any violation of this policy should immediately report it to company management, human resources, or corporate security, and should directly contact proper law enforcement authorities if there is an immediate serious threat to the safety or health of themselves or others.

Most people who are violent exhibit warning signs. If you see a number of the following signs (not just one) you need to complain to your manager or HR immediately.

Warning Signs

Every case of workplace violence by employees has been thoroughly studied. The vast majority of perpetrators had long years of service with their companies. Usually they felt they had been denied a promotion they thought they were entitled to, or they had been terminated. In virtually every case, the perpetrators made threats beforehand. Violent people also share these characteristic behaviors, which are usually clustered:

- Threatening and Disturbing Behavior
  - direct and indirect threats
  - mood swings, depression, bizarre statements, delusions of persecution
- History of Violence
  - domestic violence, verbal abuse, antisocial activities
- Romantic Obsession
  - physical or romantic obsession
- Substance Abuse
  - trouble with alcohol or drug addiction
- Depressive Behavior
  - self-destructive behavior
  - loner behavior or isolating themselves from others
  - unkempt physical appearance, despair, sluggish decision-making
- Pathological Blamer
  - failure to accept responsibility for their actions
  - constantly blaming coworkers, employer, government, the system

- Impaired Ability to Function
  - ➤ poor impulse control
- Obsession with Weapons
  - ➤ ownership of gun or gun collection, combined with antisocial behavior
  - ➤ fascination with shooting skills or weapon-related activity
- Personality Disorder
  - ➤ antisocial or borderline personality disorders
  - ➤ irritable, aggressive behavior; involvement in disputes or fights with others
  - ➤ stealing or destroying property with little remorse
  - ➤ borderline personality: shows moodiness, instability, impulsive action, easily agitated

If you believe that you're working with someone who is creating an unsafe working condition, you should not hesitate to complain. Your safety should be a priority.

What to Say and What Not to Say

There's a wide spectrum of situations that constitute harassment, and an even wider array of responses that you may need to employ to combat it. But the most effective thing you can do is to nip it in the bud, long before it advances to something like a quid pro quo situation. You can do this through invoking the company policy and making clear that you have been the object of unwanted attention. Do so by taking these steps:

1. **Record-keeping.** First, document incidents of this kind. Keep a log of workplace behavior—the more documentation of facts, the better. But be sure that you only document the

facts of someone's behavior, not your conclusions, biases, or assumptions. Write, for example, "John said: 'You have great legs' ten times this week," not "John sexually harassed me." The more details you have, the better.

2. **Be specific.** Don't go to your supervisor, your boss's boss, or HR and say things such as "John doesn't respect me," "John's discriminating against me," or "John's mean to me" without the facts to back up your statements. You have a right to your feelings, certainly, and many times your gut feelings can be correct, but your feelings do not help you make your complaint valid.

3. **Speak up.** Tell your harasser to stop. This is not necessarily an easy thing to do, but often it proves to be the most powerful tool in your arsenal. You have a better chance of making the harassment stop if you do this early on and disrupt the pattern of harassment before it becomes a habit by the other person. Just do it. It's detrimental to let things intensify past offensive pictures, cartoons, off-color jokes, or comments about your appearance that make you feel uncomfortable.

4. **Best practices.** When you do complain, use the 1-2-3 Go! format outlined in Chapter 1. Starting and ending with appreciation, along with having a specific request in mind, can turn your request into something useful, instead of just whining. A request can be something simple, such as "I want the behavior to stop." It doesn't have to be complicated.

When you confront your harasser, he or she may try to make a joke of it or claim ignorance of the behavior. Be ready with your record of incidents. Be willing to stand up for yourself and for your own needs. Be clear that you are uncomfortable with these actions and you need them to stop. And keep in mind that, no matter how embarrassing it may feel to bring this up, no matter what kind of reaction you get, you deserve to feel safe and respected at work.

It is crucially important to tell your harasser to stop the behavior and to speak up as soon as possible in order to try to resolve the situation. Doing so tells the person exactly what behavior is unwelcome and what to do to stop it. If the situation doesn't change, you have the advantage of having brought it out into the open. Of course, certain kinds of "unwanted behavior" may fit the legal definition of sexual harassment. Identifying it as such gives you the ammunition you may need later if you decide to bring a legal case against your harasser and/or the company.

When confronting your harasser, it is best to make your request in a clear and unemotional manner. You are asking for a simple and reasonable behavioral change. Think of it as a "pass-the-salt" moment. Your words need to clearly and directly describe the unwanted behavior and then express your own wish to have it stop. Don't cloud the moment with emotion—it could muddy the waters or even exacerbate the situation. Just use a tone that you would use to make the most mundane request—and keep your cool. Review and use the 1-2-3 Go! format, which means that after you've said your piece, you leave. You've done what you needed to do.

When Things Get Serious

If the behavior does not stop, it's time to take things to a higher level: You must consider going over your boss's head.

Anytime you do something like this, of course, you risk wasting political capital. Everyone has only so much capital at work (goodwill that you don't have to earn but that just comes from being given the benefit of the doubt), and any time you go around your boss, you do risk making him or her angry. But sometimes you have to take that risk, especially if it's your boss that's harassing you or asking you to lie. You should also go over your boss's head if you've repeatedly asked him or her to make sure that the behavior stops and nothing has happened. In that case, you need to go to your boss's boss or to HR.

You should do the same in these situations that you've done all along. Describe the specific incidents of the behaviors. (Remember that record you're keeping?) Tell the boss's boss or the HR rep how you've handled the situation so far, and recount in a rational, not emotional, way your harasser's reaction and his or her disregard of your request. Ask pointedly what can and will be done on your behalf and how soon you can expect to see action.

If the behavior you're dealing with is clearly out of bounds, it's important to act quickly and decisively. Don't second-guess yourself, don't be too embarrassed to act, don't tell yourself things are not so bad. Share your concerns with someone in authority and let him or her decide. Bottom line: You have a right to be safe at work and to be treated with respect. If that's not happening, outside help may be the only way to go.

The following are situations that most clearly demonstrate a problem that appears to cross legal or moral lines:

1. You're being pressured to have sex in order to keep your job, get a promotion, or earn a raise.
2. You have clear and compelling evidence that you are being discriminated against based on one of the conditions cited earlier in this chapter.

3. You have evidence you are being retaliated against because of some action you took with regard to your employer.
4. You have been physically threatened or have good reason to believe a coworker is contemplating violence.

In cases like these, don't wait to take action—that has consequences of its own, including making it harder to pursue a legal solution later. It could also embolden your harasser or, in a worst-case scenario, it could place people's lives in danger. Even if you end up finding out that you were wrong and feel that you blew things out of proportion, even if you can't put together a legal case although you feel the behavior was damaging, you can take pride in the fact that you followed your own instincts and cared enough to act, on your own behalf or on the behalf of others. Not everyone can say that.

Sample Script

CARLA: Chief, I need to talk to you about something that has been happening during my training.

CHIEF: Sure, come on in. How's it going?

CARLA: Not well. It's hard to do a good job when I'm being subjected to different standards.

CHIEF: What do you mean?

CARLA: I appreciate how busy you are and I wouldn't come to you if I had any other choice. (Offers appreciation and understanding.) I'm the only recruit that they videotape during those runs. I'm the only recruit who is asked to redo my scuba suit try-on's every day and the only recruit who has to be ready at 6:00 A.M. I've kept a log of all the different ways I've been treated. Here is your copy. I need this different treatment to stop. (Specific request for a specific change in behavior.) I understand that the training function is not part of your job, but I really needed you to know what's going on. (Offers more understanding and appreciation.)

CHIEF: Thank you for letting me know. I'm going to look into this.

CARLA: When might I expect to hear back from you?

Make sure to document this conversation with your boss and all other conversations that you've had about your complaints. Be sure to ask for a specific time when he or she will get back to you.

Boss Communication Don'ts	Boss Communication Dos
Allow someone to trample on your rights.	*Know your rights.*
Complain with conclusions.	*Assert specifics.*
Fail to document.	*Document events and conversations.*

Chapter 5

How to Complain about People or Work

Tom Maynard jammed his headphones onto his curly-haired head and fumed. If he had to listen to one more day of Steve Speakerphone's harangues to customers, other employees—and even his mother for heaven's sake—he'd throw things. The only way to find peace and quiet so that he could concentrate on his own work was to turn up the volume on the music in his own headphones, not something he wanted to do today. He needed peace and quiet! Whoever came up with the idea of cubes leading to teamwork and esprit de corps should be shot. He'd sell his soul for a private office.

Complaints about Another Employee

Complaints about another employee run the gamut from lip smackers to slackers, know-it-alls to interrupters. Oddly enough, however, most complaints seem to come from employees who can't concentrate because someone else talks too loud or constantly uses her speakerphone. The consensus in the March 2006

Randstad survey of 2,318 employed adults on the topic of workplace etiquette revealed that:

- 45 percent said condescending tones were the worst
- 37 percent found public reprimands at work particularly irritating
- 32 percent of employees listed "loud talkers" as one of their biggest pet peeves in the office

After that, micromanaging struck a nerve with 34 percent of the respondents, even more than cell phones ringing (30 percent), use of speakerphones in public areas (22 percent), and using PDAs (personal digital assistants) during meetings (9 percent). And 11 percent of those polled were annoyed when colleagues engage in personal conversations in the workplaces.

As you can see, you're not alone in your complaints!

Handling It Yourself

When I tried to counsel Tom, in the scenario above, about what to say, it became clear that one of his problems was that he'd never bothered to create a relationship with Steve. Trying to bring up an issue such as use of a speakerphone with someone you have no relationship with is difficult.

Ironically, Steve sat just a few cubes away, but Tom had decided early on that he didn't like Steve, so he avoided any contact. Not a good tactic, since you never know when you might need to be able to communicate with your coworker.

As an extrovert, it's always hard for me to imagine how someone can just ignore someone they see every day, but Tom was an introvert, an engineer who came in every morning and was focused and "on task," ready to get the work done.

> ## "We need to talk"
>
> Create a relationship before there's a problem. If you're new to a group, or new people come in, invite people for lunch or coffee, even if it's just a break in the company cafeteria. If you're of the opposite gender and you're worried that someone will misinterpret your actions, invite a same-sex person to come with you. When you develop the relationship first, it becomes much easier to ask for what you need later.
>
> Look for how you can help that person. Try to find out what he's looking for in his job and how you can help him get it. Obviously, you don't want to help people to the extinction of your own work, but you can do small favors that may win you big points. Having a reputation as being helpful will serve you in the long run.

Although this is a book about having conversations with your boss, I always recommend that you start by having a conversation with the offending employee first. Bosses love people who can handle their own relationships and loathe getting involved in these kinds of issues unless it's absolutely necessary.

While it's valid to speak up when you just can't get your work done, it's an important social skill to make sure that you do so in the most productive way possible. "Likability" is just as important to your career success as any kind of technical skill, perhaps more so.

According to a *Harvard Business Review* study published in 2005, people would rather work with someone they like, even if that person is incompetent. Most people in the survey picked that option over working with someone unlikable that they didn't like. Interestingly, how people valued competence, the study found, depended upon how likable the participants found the coworker.

It's human nature not to like a whiner, so raise your complaints sparingly and skillfully but by all means raise them if your coworkers' behavior is interfering with your getting your own work done.

Complain for the Right Reason

Getting your own work done should be the criteria you use in deciding when and where to complain. If you develop a reputation as someone who is just constantly pointing out others' flaws for no good reason that will not serve you well. Consider the employee of one of my clients, Esmeralda.

* * *

Esmeralda was a chronic complainer, someone who was also a know-it-all. She was new to the law firm and thought that it was her job to provide feedback about everything—telling people how to make the coffee, how to write briefs, how to comb their hair. Now feedback is good, but it's best to wait until you get the lay of the land if you're new to an organization. Esmeralda had no compunctions about giving feedback to anyone—including the senior partner of the firm. She did, however, work hard and had a good legal mind, so the firm wanted to save her as an employee and brought me in to coach her.

* * *

It was tough to get Esmeralda to realize that not everyone needed her advice! It took a lot of feedback from me about the various complaints I'd received from other people about her to convince Esmeralda that she needed to dial down the feedback. "Ask yourself, first" I counseled her, "whether what you're telling them has any impact on your performance or the performance of your team. If it doesn't, keep your mouth shut."

*　　*　　*

It took time, but eventually Esmeralda learned to wait and think before she spoke.

*　　*　　*

I'm not advising you to never speak up, just to make sure that there's a business reason for doing so and that it's *your* business. Otherwise, stay out of the business of unsolicited advice and wait until someone asks for your opinion.

With Tom and Mr. Speakerphone, however, Tom clearly needed to speak up, since Steve's behavior affected his own performance. An inability to get your work done because of someone else's behavior is always a legitimate complaint.

When you do have a conflict such as the Tom/Steve Speakerphone debacle, and decide that it's worth the risk to speak up and complain, follow these steps:

Assume positive intent. Rascals abound, no question. But it's always a good idea to assume that people are clueless and have no idea how much their behavior is bothering you. Most people, in fact, are very distracted these days—not necessarily full-blown ADD (Attention Deficit Disorder) but what psychiatrist and author Edward Hallowell calls a "severe case of modern life." All of that distraction makes us very self-centered in the sense that we're focusing on what's right in front of us instead of what other people around us need. We're too overwhelmed to think about our effect on other people's needs; we're having enough trouble getting through the day meeting our own needs.

Record the specifics of the problematic behavior. When you do identify a problem that you need to talk to a coworker about, spend some time writing it out until you can turn your complaint into a behaviorally specific request, as identified in Chapter 1.

Use the 1-2-3 Go! format.
1. Steve, I understand how passionate you are about your job.
2. However, I just can't concentrate when you use the speakerphone. Could you please not use it when I'm at work?
3. I appreciate your doing this for me.

Try humor. If someone fails to comply with your request, I'm a big fan of using humor, instead of upping the ante and getting madder. If, after a request, for example, Steve continues shouting into the speakerphone, Tom could tell him that clearly, he needs a bit of reminding. He could bring in a Nerf ball and inform Steve that he's going to playfully toss it over his cube whenever he's talking too loud.

Solving a situation like this can be viewed as annoying, but try to reframe the situation as just another chance to improve your conflict skills. Just like exercise, using your skills is a good chance to gain conflict "muscle."

Sample Script   *"We need to talk"*

TOM: Hi Steve, do you have a minute?

STEVE: Sure.

TOM: I'm sure that you're not aware of this problem and that if you were, you'd want to do something about it. I understand how busy you are. (Starts with understanding and appreciation.)

I have trouble working when you speak into your speakerphone so loudly. I would really appreciate it if you would use your handset instead or perhaps a headphone if you need to have your hands free when you're talking. (Makes a behaviorally specific request.)

I really appreciate your doing this for me. I want us to have a good working relationship. Thanks.

Tom then needs to walk off to give Steve time to absorb his request.

If Steve doesn't stop, Tom needs to up the ante. The first tactic is to try humor. Such a script would look like this:

TOM: Steve, I noticed that you've been having a hard time remembering to use the handset instead of the speakerphone. You said that you'd be willing to do this so I'm going to try to help you remember. I have my new handy Nerf ball here, and I'm just going to toss it over whenever the volume is too loud. I got one for you too in case you have the same problem with me being too loud. Thanks so much. I really appreciate your doing this for me. I know that we both need to get our work done since there's so much going on right now.

After this conversation, Tom should e-mail Steve his thanks and briefly outline what Steve has done to fix the problem. Tom should do this every time he speaks to Steve, so that he will have a record of his attempts to solve the problem when he talks to his boss.

When to Complain to Your Boss

If you do decide that you need to go to your boss with your complaint, be sure that you've documented all your attempts to talk with your coworker. Use the format suggested in the last chapter of documenting conversations after you have them. Send an e-mail or memo to your coworker confirming what you told him and his response.

When you do talk with your boss, pick your time and place. Timing is so important in all of these challenging boss conversations, but even more so when you have to bring up an unresolved problem with a coworker. As I mentioned, bosses hate getting involved in these kinds of disputes, so you don't want to bring them up the day before the quarterly reports are due, when he's jet lagged from his trip to Bangkok, or when she's just returned from maternity leave. Pick a time when your boss seems fairly relaxed and there's no crisis in the works.

Be sure to start with an understanding statement so that you validate how busy you know your boss always is and how much you've tried to resolve this issue by yourself. Don't require your boss to read all of your documentation, but be sure to have it out, noticeably in your hand while you're talking to her in order to let her know that it's available if she wants to read it.

Stress that you know she has a lot on her plate, and you greatly appreciate her taking the time to deal with this matter, as you really can't get your work done with this much noise, harassment, sloth, or whatever the case may be.

When you do talk to your boss, follow these rules:

- Focus on the behavior not the person
- Specifically describe the problem behavior
- Suggest a solution—even if it's just that the behavior stop
- Offer an understanding or apology for not being able to handle this yourself

If you follow this format your boss should be ready to listen to you and absorb what you're trying to say.

Sample Script

TOM: Ms. Boss, I'm sorry to bother you and I know how busy you are but I really need to speak with you about Steve Speakerphone. (Starts with appreciation and understanding.)

MS. BOSS: Yes?

TOM: Steve has a habit of carrying on every conversation over his speakerphone. As you're aware, my cube is right next to his and I am having trouble focusing when he talks so loudly on his speakerphone. (Specifically describes the behavior.) I've talked to him about it at least six times. Here's my documentation of our conversations. (Documents that he's tried to get the behavior to stop.) I really can't concentrate and get my work done when he does this. Could you please talk with him and get this behavior to stop? (Suggests a specific solution.) I really appreciate your taking the time to solve this problem. (Adds more appreciation and understanding.)

How to Complain about Your Boss—to Your Boss

First of all, even if you believe you have a good reason to offer criticism to your boss, stop and think first. Most people don't like criticism, and your boss is no exception. You need to tread very carefully here.

Consider the plight of one of the employees of one of my clients. Mark had worked for a nonprofit for ten years. He had a reputation as a solid employee, although a bit of a know-it-all. When he lost out on a promotion, he took it out on his immediate boss—even though the boss had not been involved in the promotional decision. He savaged his boss in his 360 review of his boss's performance.

Even though such reviews are supposed to be confidential, his boss came right to him with the results and challenged every one of his statements. Mark was shocked but tried to respond as best he could. The relationship went downhill from there.

The problem was that Mark—totally apart from the 360 debacle—had a reputation for being a "got you" person. He loved to point out people's flaws in front of other people. In a meeting with the director of operations, for example, he scathingly criticized her new manual in front of everyone. When someone sent out an e-mail to the team asking for input, he responded on his own instead of waiting for the team consensus.

This left Mark vulnerable to his boss's feedback that he was "not a team player" and that he lacked good people skills.

No one likes to be told that he is not good at what he does, that he has made a mistake in front of others, or that he's incompetent. If you're going to offer criticism or feedback to your boss, your touch must be light and careful.

If you're absolutely, positively sure that you should proceed, follow these rules:

- Do it in private. Follow that old management rubric: praise in public, criticize in private.
- Don't be generic. Telling someone that she's a horrible boss doesn't help her or you.
- Focus on one specific behavior at a time.
- Focus on behavior, not the person. *Be behaviorally specific.*
- State your intention. Why are you telling this person this? In order to avoid being seen as a know-it-all, make sure that you have a clear and business-related reason.

"We need to talk"

If you're complaining just to show how smart you are and/or to show your boss up, that's not a good reason. What you need to do instead is to state a business-focused reason—such as that it will help improve the performance or profits of the team, that another employee or customer has been complaining about this and that you thought your boss should know, or something else that links your message to the good of the whole.

- Focus on something positive. Every boss has his or her good points. Be sure that you mention these, along with the problem areas; you don't want to just focus on the problem without something positive.
- Avoid loaded words or labeling of someone's behavior, which is only likely to escalate matters in an unhelpful way. Focus on specific examples of the behavior that you want changed and

specific requests for change. Avoid big subjects; focus on small steps—what behavioral psychologists call "approximations." What that means is rewarding any small progress toward the goal that you want and ignoring lapses.

Think twice and then think again about what your real intentions are and what you hope to gain by stepping into this particular swamp.

Mark, for example, talked to a number of other employees about what he'd claimed was his boss's plagiarism. Using words such as "plagiarism" and talking with other employees first can only create harm if you've set out to critique your boss. None of us like criticism, but we especially bristle when it is reported secondhand. In most workplaces, the gossip train speeds faster than the Internet.

"We need to talk"

MARK: I need to talk to you about this legislative report.

JOHN: Okay.

MARK: I noticed that on page two we (Approaching the issue as a joint problem to be solved, instead of criticism or labeling it as "plagiarism.") need to add a citation for this material.

JOHN: Okay.

MARK: I also noticed a few other places where we'd neglected this and I wasn't sure of the source. It seems that we need to add citations on pages nine, twelve, and fourteen also. I've marked the places; could you please add what we need there?

JOHN: Sure, I'll take a look and do that.

As usual, Mark should document this conversation by sending a confirming e-mail to John and thanking him for talking about the problem.

Complaining about Work

Oddly, most people seem to have trouble at work because of one of the relationship issues outlined in this chapter, not because of the work itself. You may, however, have the need at some point to complain about what you're actually doing.

If so, many of the general principles cited here still apply. In addition, do your homework. Be sure to be specific when complaining about your current work and what would make your work more satisfying. If you're not good at your current job, however, it's unlikely that your boss will be amenable to changing your work assignments. Take these steps:

- Figure out how to do your current work well, even if you believe that it's boring or beneath you. As Martin Luther King, Jr., advised, "If you're a street sweeper, be the Michelangelo of street sweepers."
- After that, go back and look at your original job description and why you were hired. Are you doing something substantially different from what you thought you would be doing? If so, document the differences.
- If you have a good HR department, you might consider consulting with them about your job description, classifications, and the work that you've actually wound up doing. Don't criticize your boss when you do this; simply inquire so that you have the information that you need.
- Ask around and try to find out what your coworkers are actually working on. If what they're working on is substantially different from what you're doing, and you're at the same level, document that before you go in to speak to your boss.
- Do your research to find out what you want instead of what you're currently doing. Come in armed with a plan and suggestions that are realistic. Bosses are human beings too. Most of them don't like to disappoint other people. Try to put together something that you know will work. Consider the needs of the business as well as your own needs.

- Try to phrase your request in a way that shows you understand that your job needs to make business sense. Put the needs of the business first, and it will be harder for your boss to consider saying no.

Take Jennifer, for example, a public relations specialist for one of my clients. Her new boss changed her work assignments to include standard press releases, something Jennifer hadn't done for years and something that she considered to be outside the scope of her current job description.

While new bosses have a right to change your job or assignments based on the realities of the business, sometimes they just don't realize how much they've changed what you're doing and how difficult that can make your work.

Jennifer did her homework, documenting the percentage of her time that she'd spent on press releases before and after her new boss, and the years she'd spent doing more substantive work.

She then picked a good time to approach her boss about the switch.

Sample Script

JENNIFER: Ms. New Boss, do you have a minute?

MS. NEW: Sure, I'm in a lull right now.

JENNIFER: I appreciate (Starts with appreciation and understanding.) that it takes awhile to get the lay of the land around here, but I have some concerns about my new assignments.

MS. NEW: Oh really?

JENNIFER: There's no reason for you to know this (Assumes positive intent.) but I really haven't done standard press releases for years. I've been concentrating on client relations and special events. I've really invested a lot of time into learning that arena, both by working directly with clients and by going to seminars. I've gone back and tracked my hours over the past two years before you came, and you can see what I was doing then. I'm concerned that if I go back to focusing on press releases, it will not be in the firm's best interest to use my skills in that way. (Focusing on the needs of the business, not just her own personal needs.)

MS. NEW: Oh really? I wasn't aware of that.

JENNIFER: I'm wondering if you could take another look at the new assignments and reconsider. I've made a list of all the new client events that I'm aware of and added suggestions for how I think my skills could be useful on those projects.

MS. NEW: What a good idea. I'll take a look and get back to you.

JENNIFER: Thanks. I really appreciate your being so flexible about changing your mind and being willing to do that. (Ends with more appreciation.)

MS. NEW: No problem.

Boss Communication Don'ts	Boss Communication Dos
Attach a negative broad label.	Ask for small, specific changes.
Talk with others.	Talk with the person who has the power to solve the problem.
Go to your boss first.	Go to the person who is engaged in the behavior.
Whine over every issue.	Solve your own problems whenever possible.

"We need to talk"

Chapter 6

How to Find Out What's Really Going On

CHANDRA LEE TOILED through college and law school in order to end up exactly where she was. Yet doubt nagged at her soul. She'd never cracked the code for the old "boys' club" in her firm. She'd worked hard and made partner, but she knew that she'd been fast-tracked because of the color of her skin: they needed better numbers for important government contracts. The signs were subtle: informal meetings to which she'd not been invited, after-hours drinking she never heard about until too late, work assigned to others, and so on. She wanted to be part of the club but it seemed as if she'd missed the secret handshake.

She had absolutely, positively no idea about how to find out what was really going on. *Do you?*

Why You Should Care

Perhaps you're one of those people who are extensively focused on "task" and really just don't understand why you should care about "office gossip," "politics," or being "in the know." If so, listen up. You really do need to care. Sad but true: most people are not promoted based on work alone; it's a combination of work and relationship skills, relationships being most important. How will you know that you should be angling for a promotion if you don't even know that a promotion is coming up? And how would you know that a big merger is coming up and you're going to be merged out of a job if you don't know about the merger? Navigate toward this information like a heat-seeking missile; search as if your career depended upon it. Most likely it does.

Unwritten Rules Are Important

In addition to specifics about upcoming events—mergers, acquisitions, and the like—most people also need to be in the know about "unwritten rules." Unwritten rules are the types of things that everyone "in the know" seems aware of but you aren't. Few things are more important than being aware of these rules.

There's nothing necessarily dysfunctional about organizations having unwritten rules; every organization needs to have them, or the official rulebook would be thousands of pages long. Yet some groups have more than others, and every group has different norms about how these rules are passed along.

The ideal, of course, is to have both formal and informal mentorship programs through which these rules are passed along. However, in my experience, most organizations don't do a very good job of imparting these subtle norms of behavior.

Unwritten rules can be minor things, such as "don't drink out of that generic-looking coffee cup because it's the boss's" or big things, such as "this is the kind of work that's really valued here, no matter what people say." If you haven't received the kind of mentoring you deserve, your job is to take the proverbial bull by the horns and find out anyway.

How to Find Out about Unwritten Rules

The best way to find out about unwritten rules is to ask questions constantly and seek feedback about your own behavior. These questions need to be asked early and often. Start with a tee-up, or you risk appearing rude or brusque, but get in the habit of asking, directly and indirectly, about rules of behavior and social norms.

Good ways of starting such conversations with your boss or others (after the tee-up) are questions such as:

- What do you wish you'd known about this place when you just started here?
- What kinds of things do you think most people don't seem to understand about working here?
- What, if anything, do you notice that I don't seem to understand about working here that you wish I did?
- My experience is that every workplace seems to have different ideas about what is or is not okay for people to do. What kinds of things are unique to this workplace?

If you ask these kinds of questions, you'll have less of a chance of being caught by surprise. Make it a habit to ask different people for this kind of feedback.

How to Find Out What's on the Horizon

Information about reorganizations, new executives, new owners, and the like is always known by someone—your job is to find out who has this information. In fact, there's usually a busybody in every office, plant, or shop who always seems to know everything first. This may be the boss's assistant, or an office clerk, but they have the gift of gab as well as the gift of encouraging others to talk. You would do well to befriend this person, no matter what you might think of his or her personal style.

The other way is to learn to ask open-ended questions of people in the know, such as your boss or other people who always hear the news before anyone else. Open-ended questions are those that do not presume the answers. Questions that presume the answers are those that are frequently leading questions that can be answered yes or no.

Examples of leading questions include the following:

- Don't you just love working here?
- Do you know what's happening in the executive suite?
- Have you heard about the upcoming merger?

The rule of thumb is that if it's a question that will lead to a one-word—yes or no—answer, it's a leading question that you should avoid. Not because there's anything inherently wrong with such questions, but because they simply won't give you as much information as you really need to find out what's going on.

Instead, you want to get in the habit of asking questions that encourage dialogue, questions that start with *how*, *who*, *what*, *where*, or *when*. If, for example, you've heard rumors about new owners but don't have any good intelligence on the situation, you can start asking your boss or others *how* they feel about the new changes that are coming along, without specifying exactly what you mean. (There's always change.) You can always ask people to speculate, also, by asking them *what* changes they're likely to see coming along in the next year.

Change is a constant in most organizations these days so asking about it will serve you well. Other good dialogue starters:

- Who do you see as rising stars in the organization?
- What surprised you most about your job when you started here?
- Where did you get your start in this industry?
- When have you felt most insecure in this business?

If you're in the habit of having these kinds of conversations (after you do a few tee-ups, of course, about the weather, the local sports team, or the lousy plant coffee) you'll automatically be in the know when changes come along, as well as understanding unwritten rules when necessary.

Be sure to start with a tee-up so that that your conversations don't seem too blunt or direct, which sometimes makes people uncomfortable—once that happens, you won't get the information that you need. As discussed in Chapter 1, tee-ups are neutral topics of conversation that help you get the ball rolling.

What if you're striving to find out something more specific? For example, my client Val had constant run-ins with her new boss, as did all of the other people in her department. In fact, the tension escalated until everyone in her department was scrambling for other jobs. Val couldn't imagine how the new boss was keeping her job when everyone had gone to *her* boss to complain. There has to be something going on that's protecting her, I kept insisting: most likely money or sex (those being the two most common protective factors in any office). "You need to do some intelligence gathering," I instructed her.

Sure enough, when her boss left four months later, so did the boss above her, and the affair came out.

How could Val have found out before this? Again, the office know-it-all is the best source. Although spreading rumors and gossip is never a good idea, sometimes you really do need to know what's going on in order to save your own sanity.

Office Politics and Social Skills

Many of you are probably still resistant to the idea of pursuing office politics. You're sure, like Chandra, that you can get by on good work alone.

Beware. Many studies by social psychologists show that people who find and keep the best jobs also have the best social skills. Study after study has shown that social skills matter more than technical skills or good work alone. Peruse Daniel Goleman's book, *Social Intelligence*, if you're not familiar with this literature.

Politics exist in every organization—look at your own family dynamics. In most families, there are things that everyone knows not to tell Grandma or Aunt Mabel. Similarly, there are some things you have to make sure you tell your mom because she'll freak if she hears them first from your sister.

Workplaces operate the same way. In order to be linked-in, you have to be in the know. In order to be in the know you have to have good social skills and use them—even when you don't want to.

Still unconvinced? Look at this list of traits that recruiters look for in business school candidates:

- Communication and interpersonal skills
- Original and visionary thinking
- Leadership potential
- Ability to work well within a team
- Analytical and problem-solving skills

While you have to be smart and good at what you do, brushing up on your social skills isn't optional—especially in today's team-oriented environment.

"We need to talk"

Social scientists have identified different kinds of social skills, but many are based on reading social cues—including reading faces to tell when someone's reacting to what you're saying and why. Most people develop these skills when they are babies, but for those who don't or can't, there's actually a name for their lack of ability to read social cues—it's called *dyssemia*—and you can actually find books and classes that tell you how to do it.

Performance Is Not Enough

Don't think that you can just put your head down and do your work. Most people are hired for what they know, and fired—or fail to advance—because of who they are. If people don't like you, you won't advance at work and won't get what you want.

The good news is that once you have the intention to be good at office politics, it's really not rocket science. All it requires is some rather old-fashioned values, such as being interested in other people and caring about what they care about. Most people are interesting if we take enough time to get to know them, and most of us can learn to care about what other people care about if we put enough value on what they need and want.

You're in It Together

Other social science research points to the fact that we're really hard-wired for intimacy, even at the level of our brain chemistry. Interestingly enough, it's in our genes. Our ancestors were more likely to survive the travails of floods, famine, and outside dangers if they were part of a group. Those people drawn to groups were more likely to pass on their DNA.

We're really not different from our forebears. We're wired for connection: studies show that most of us become despondent without enough of it. Although certainly people vary in the amount of connection they need, we all need some.

People with good social skills know instinctively—or through what they've learned—to monitor how they act with different groups. Social scientists call these people high self-monitors; people who have difficulty with this skill are called low self-monitors. People with this social skill are able to change the way they interact in a group, depending on how the group is behaving and what they learn based on the group's norms. People with low self-monitoring have only one way of behaving, no matter what the group.

What you do doesn't have to be world changing or difficult. Take the time to get to know your coworkers until you find out what they need and want, and then try to help them—even in some small way—get what they want.

Never underestimate the power of flattery—although focus on something that you truly believe; most people can spot a false compliment. Look for the good and praise it. Interestingly enough, most of us don't do this enough. John Gottman's research on happy marriages shows that a five-to-one ratio of complementary to critical remarks is what it takes to cancel out the criticism. In my experience of working with hundreds of clients, the workplace is no different.

Frequently, workers with poor social skills include not only the idiot who keeps telling a sexist joke, even though he's just been to sexual harassment training, but also the worker who criticizes everything and thinks that he'll earn points for pouncing on someone's flaws.

Consider Dan, who worked for a marketing and advertising firm that I counseled. Everyone agreed that his work was superior—his designs superb and his ads creative. But he was brusque with clients and coworkers, frequently seeming to enjoy pointing out problems before anyone else even cared. While the firm tolerated him for years because of his work, when the firm merged with another agency, and they were forced to cut designers, they found a way to merge Dan out of the deal, taking pains to keep less talented coworkers that they simply liked better.

Sample Script

CHANDRA: Mr. Boss, do you have a minute?

MR. BOSS: Sure.

CHANDRA: Wow, it sure looks like we're going to have another big storm. (Starts with a soft tee-up.) I know that you like to go up to your condo in Vail every weekend; are you planning on heading up tonight? Looks as if it's going to be a bad one.

MR. BOSS: Luckily, not tonight. We were up last weekend. This weekend, I have to catch up on work.

CHANDRA: Yes, I know the feeling; I have to prepare for the big XYZ trial next month. You know how much I appreciate working here but I'm wondering if there's a way that I could be more connected to what's going on.

MR. BOSS: I'm not sure what you mean.

CHANDRA: When, for example, the XYZ merger happened, I had no idea it was even in the works until the official public announcement. I'm wondering if there's any way that I could find out about these things before they happen.

MR. BOSS: Well, you know, it just takes time . . .

CHANDRA: (Persisting.) I notice that you, David, and Terry frequently go out for coffee on Tuesday mornings. I don't want to crash your club but I'm wondering if I could join you periodically.

MR. BOSS: I don't see why not. I'll let you know the next time we go.

CHANDRA: Thanks. I'd be grateful. I just feel as if I could do a better job for the firm if I were a bit more in the loop. Speaking of which, I'm wondering what you're thinking about the new Executive Committee elections coming up. I really haven't been able to decide who I'm voting for, since I really don't know the partners in Minneapolis all that well. I really respect your judgment and I'm wondering what you're thinking about the pros and cons of each candidate.

MR. BOSS: Well, Jerry, for example . . .

Boss Communication Don'ts	Boss Communication Dos
Assume that information doesn't matter.	*Keep up with what's going on.*
Be afraid to ask questions.	*Become an expert at asking the right questions.*
Blurt out important questions.	*Use soft tee-ups.*
Ignore office politics.	*Know that politics count.*

Chapter 7

How to Find Out What Your Boss Really Thinks

GLEN CONNER READ the e-mail from his boss and swiveled around in his chair. Another obscure message: what the hell did "proceed as planned on the Banner project" mean? They had no plans as far as he could tell. He'd pleaded and nagged for some time on Gail's calendar for weeks to no avail. She thought her team knew what they were doing, but Glen had no idea. Gail spent her weeks on the road, traveling to see clients all over the world. Her brief pit stops in the office revolved around meeting with the other sales VPs. Her staff referred to her as "Casper" since she'd become a ghost in the office. Why hadn't anyone ever warned him that mind reading was required for this job?

He needed to talk with her but he had absolutely, positively, no idea what to say.

How to Graciously Ask the Tough Questions

Glen's dilemma is common these days. With work-at-home options, travel, and endless meetings jamming bosses' calendars, finding out what they really think or want has disappeared. No longer can a hapless employee expect to be told what to do with a detailed list and expert follow-up. More often, you're required to just know or figure it out for yourself and expect to pay for any mistakes.

Staying on top of what your boss wants and needs requires you to initiate the tough questions. You can't wait for her to tell you what to do, unless you're lucky enough to have a stay-at-home boss. Instead, you need to find out what she wants before she wants it. While the previous chapter was about finding out about the company in general, this chapter is about finding out specifically what's on your boss's mind.

Ask the Right Questions

The art then becomes, asking the right question at the right time. Ideally, you need to set up regular meetings with your boss before you need them, at least once a month, but perhaps as often as once a week if your job requires fast turnaround and timelines.

Should your boss be the one to instigate these meetings? Ideally, but, of course, there is no such thing as the ideal boss. Therefore, you have to take the lead.

In those periodic meetings, make it clear that you relentlessly seek and welcome feedback and direction. Ask questions such as the following:

- What did you think the strengths and weaknesses of XYZ report that I just turned in were?
- What's most useful about the work I've been doing for you?
- What's least useful?

- How can I help you meet your goals better?
- What do you know about the workload between now and the end of the year?

If you're in the habit of regularly asking these kinds of questions, your boss won't be surprised if and when you have to ask the tough questions.

Raising Risky Issues

When you do need to ask something that you consider risky in some way, use this format:

- A soft tee-up
- An open-ended question
- Appreciation and thanks for her candor

As we've mentioned elsewhere in this book, tee-ups are important for many business conversations. While no one appreciates a person who goes on and on without getting to the point, a person who blurts out something challenging becomes equally avoided. Letting someone know your intention in asking a tough question is a good way to start, as is reminding her that your goal always is to do the best possible job for your organization and to make her life easier.

Breaking Down Questions

When you do have to move on to the question itself, sometimes you'll be more successful if you break it down to bite-sized pieces. A big leap into the subject can be intimidating to some people—especially those who like to avoid conflict. If you want to find out whether you'll have a job after the merger, for example, start out by asking your boss what pros and cons she sees to the merger. Avoid asking her what she thinks of the merger in general, as this may lead her to just repeat the company line. Pros and cons may help her reveal something more. After you've given her a chance to talk, gently try to find out more about your own position by asking questions such as these:

- I know they have a big sales force and I'm wondering, how will I fit in with that mix?
- What might I do best this year to plan for next year?
- In my year-end evaluation, we talked about my moving into the imaging group in the future; how does the merger possibly impact that idea?

Even if you ask all the right questions, you may still be puzzled as to what your boss is really thinking. The next section may provide some clues.

How to Find Out What's Really in Your Boss's Head

Sometimes you have to become a bit of a stalker with your boss. Of course, if her office is in another building, state, or, heaven forbid, country, you'll have a big problem with this. But if you're lucky enough to be in the same building as your boss, try to carefully and unobtrusively spend some time walking by her office. Befriend her assistant if you can, find out what hours she keeps, where she works out, where she gets her coffee. Running into her coming and going allows you to strengthen your relationship through casual conversation and work up to the difficult issues.

I once asked a well-known hotel executive how he found out what his notoriously difficult boss was really thinking, and he responded that he went to his boss's boss and asked him: What's my boss thinking about Y? This requires, of course, an existing and good relationship with your boss's boss, but some people through happenstance or personality fit tend to have a better relationship with someone higher up than they do with their immediate boss. If you try this tactic, be sure to include it as a casual aside, instead of something crucial, to avoid creating impossible political fallout with your own boss thinking you're doing an end-run.

What Your Boss Would Say if She Could

You may think that you have it tough these days: doing more with less, working longer hours, fewer medical and other benefits, and less direction and opportunity—but you might be surprised to learn that your boss has even more stressful problems. You may think that she is the source of your stress, but most likely, she's squeezed between her own individual work and supervising more employees. Most managers have tighter budgets and fewer people available to get things accomplished. Many organizations have cut staffs and budgets again and again, leaving mid-level managers caught in the cross-fire, trying to accomplish more with less. Sure, there are incompetent, unfriendly, and just-plain-evil bosses out there, but the majority of middle managers are reasonable people who are trying to do the best they can for the employees they supervise *and* the higher-ups.

What would most bosses say if they could speak freely to you? Based on my surveys of my clients, most of them would give you some version of the following:

"**Don't take things personally.** When I ignore you or seem distracted or uninterested in what you have to say, it's not that your great ideas don't interest me. If I act dismissive or corporate, it may be that I just don't want to admit that I don't have the money or the authority to say yes very often in the current environment." A good question when this happens is to ask, "Is this topic uncomfortable for you?" That might throw your manager off enough for him or her to open up and tell you the real problem.

"**I wish you would fight most of your own battles.** I know that you expect your boss to help you when your benefit reimbursement is messed up again by accounting or when your administrative assistant is out sick again, but I have my own battles to fight. Don't always expect me to march into accounting or HR to straighten things out for you. Let things go sometimes or try to fix things yourself."

"**Don't put me in the middle of your spats with coworkers.** I know that both of you want the trip to San Francisco or the cubicle with the window, but if I get in the middle, someone's going to be mad at me. Try to work it out yourself if at all possible and I will be grateful that you did. I'll be even more excited if you manage all this on your own without even telling me. If you can do this, when the big issues come down the pike, I'll have more energy to help you out."

"I don't want to have to monitor your every move, so don't give me a reason to." Most bosses would be willing to give you some flexibility about time and hours, as long as you do your job and get your work done. "I'd give you some flexibility to come in later or leave early as long as you do your work well and don't disappear when you know we have a crunch coming up. I can give you some slack if you manage your own workload, but not if you take advantage of my flexibility. If you do, I'll have to start watching your every move and I loathe acting like the office hall monitor."

"You know more about your work than I do and you always will. Help me out when we talk by telling me what you're working on and why. If you're confused about priorities, ask me for some guidance but don't fume silently. A written list of what you're working on before we meet would be great also, that way I don't have to panic trying to figure out what you're talking about and why."

"If I've messed up, let me know in a diplomatic way. Don't sulk without telling me why. I can't read minds, and I have a lot crowding out your concerns in my own mind right now. I may miss signals that you think are obvious. If you're pissed, please just tell me when we're not in the middle of some other crises. I'll try to do my best to listen and not get defensive."

"**I don't like surprises—especially bad news.** Let me know as far in advance as possible when you know something is not working. Almost everything can be fixed, if you let me know soon enough. Don't assume that I won't find out; I almost always will."

"**Let me know before things blow up.** If you notice something about my management style that's really damaging to you or your coworkers, please tell me. If you notice that I always ignore Susan in meetings, give me a hint that's happening."

"**Don't mess up on the obvious things.** I can save you from small mistakes but if you throw up in the CEO's lap at the holiday party, e-mail sexual jokes around the office, or falsify your expense reports, you're on your own."

Your boss may not be able to speak candidly to you, but if she could, you can be sure that she would say some version of these examples.

How to Avoid Being Blindsided

If you're having the regular no-big-deal meetings with your boss as outlined earlier, you won't have to worry about being blindsided, but one thing to add to those conversations that may help even more is a question such as "What's the most surprising company news you've had lately?" or, "It seems as if things are pretty quiet around here but sometimes I think I'm the last to know. Anything coming up that you would like to know if you were me?"

Make it a habit to ask people a clean-up question at the end of a meeting such as "Is there anything else about this subject that you would like to know if you were me?" You will be amazed what people answer in response to that particular question.

How to Tackle an Indecisive Boss

Most people either flee from conflict or approach it too aggressively. However, as discussed earlier in the book, conflict can be transformative and actually lead to better, more creative decisions than unilateral fiats or other methods. The give-and-take of creative conflict leads to innovation and gives groups the energy to fuel future work.

Taking the middle ground and using conflict positively takes time and practice. Many people wonder who causes the most problems in workplaces—those who avoid conflict or those who're too aggressive. It's the avoiders by a landslide.

For example, take Ron, a member of an executive team that I was called in to mediate. Ron had worked his way up through the ranks of a large pharmaceutical company, largely by not making waves and being nice to everyone. He'd been tapped to run a new, smaller, high-tech medical company, inheriting an executive team brimming with unproductive conflicts he'd been unable to navigate.

After I interviewed all the players I was struck with this thought: What's such a nice guy doing with so many snakes working for him? But the deeper I dug into the snake pit, the more I found the real culprit: Ron himself.

Ron was a classic conflict avoider—dodging requests for decisions on most issues, delaying others, not wanting to make the hard calls that might lower his popularity level. In classic style, his team was expressing the conflicts he repressed.

I developed a technique to work with the group that I call the "beyond list." What I find is that many groups are mired in conflicts that they have no power to resolve, just as Ron's executive team. They'd been fighting over budgets and resources and other decisions that they needed Ron to decide.

I met with the executives and asked them to work together (therapeutic in itself) on making three lists: historical issues, current issues, and "beyond issues." Beyond issues are those beyond the power of the group to resolve, though groups frequently waste their time in these disputes, unable to see the forest for the trees and realize that what they're fighting over they have no power to resolve.

After they came up with their lists, I took the details to Ron and announced that the group had worked hard but that the longest list was those that they had no power to resolve and that he needed to make decisions on the items on that list.

No dummy, Ron got the message. He didn't change overnight, and I had to continue to coach and prod him to act, but eventually, we moved into a functioning method of decision-making for his team.

Since that intervention, I've had many groups like Ron's: squabbling underlings, indecisive leader. I've since learned to look for this pattern.

You can use a version of the same technique yourself by getting the quarreling group together, making the three lists, and offering them to your leader.

Another one of my clients asked for assistance with one of their VPs. An executive with a wealth of industry knowledge and contacts, he closeted himself in his office and sent out assignments and responses on e-mails, avoiding face-to-face meetings, changing meeting times, and dodging phone calls in order to limit his decision-making. Years of frustration mounted at a corporate retreat I facilitated where the company decided that it had too many VPs. When they asked my opinion, I agreed that Mr. Indecisive should be the first to get the boot, since I'd simply had too much experience with this entrenched personality type.

If you have such a boss, you do have your work cut out for you, but try these techniques:

Power in numbers. Get together his or her direct reports, discuss the problem confidentially, and make the three lists.

Break the details into small steps. Conflict avoiders tend to be overwhelmed with large projects. If you can break the decisions down for them, you have a better chance of success.

Ask for a decision. Use the 1-2-3 Go! format, but do ask. Don't beat around the bush or sashay away from the issue. Make a specific/doable request for action.

Give them time to think. Many conflict avoiders tend to overthink things. For those of us who talk *before* thinking, this can be difficult to understand. You need to give them some time to think, but set a limit on their thinking time so that they don't think things to death.

Set a date. Make it clear that you need a decision by a certain date and be sure that you get their agreement before you leave and that the date is set.

If you follow this format, you have a good chance of pinning the conflict avoider down enough to sort out your issues.

Sample Script

GLEN: I'm sorry to interrupt but I really need to talk to you today. Is now a good time?

MS. BUSY BOSS: Well . . . if it can't wait . . .

GLEN: I know how busy you've been with your travel schedule. How did your trip to China go? (Soft tee-up.)

MS. BUSY: Oh, it was a bear. Constant meetings and with the jet lag, I could barely keep my eyes open. We did get the deal but sometimes I wonder if it's worth it. We'll see. What's up?

GLEN: I just need to check a few things about the Banner project. I'm thinking that we'll use the same format that we did for Tony Dee, but I just want to check to make sure that works for you before I go too far down that path. (Takes some initiative to figure out what might work, even though he's not sure that's what his boss had in mind.)

MS. BUSY: Well . . . to the extent I can remember that deal, I think that's a good model. Why don't you shoot me a copy of that contract and I'll take a look at it tonight?

GLEN: Great. And also, I just want to make sure that I keep doing what you want since we have so many deals going on and you're on the road so much. How was the Danger contract?

MS. BUSY: Oh, it was fine. I'm sorry, I should have told you. I just assumed that "no news was good news," you know?

GLEN: Well . . . I'm glad to hear that. One more quick thing. (Helps her understand that he's not going to meet all day with her.) I notice that you're usually in the office on Fridays and I'd like to be able to touch base with you then just to make sure that I'm on track with my work. I get in early and I know you usually do also. Could we meet at 7:30 on Fridays just until I get on top of things? I promise that I'll be fast. I'll shoot you a list of what I'm working on the day before so you can look at it before we begin and make any additions or corrections.

MS. BUSY: Sure, that should work.

Follow up with an e-mail to document your conversation.

If you have an indecisive boss, you might want to try some version of the following.

Sample Script

LARRY: Do you have a minute to talk about the results of our team meeting?

MR. AVOIDER: Can't it wait?

LARRY: I'm sorry, but it really can't. It shouldn't take long. (Doesn't back down.) The team met today to go over some of the projects we've been working on, along with deadlines. We came up with a list of things where we've decided we don't really need your help but just wanted you to be aware.

MR. AVOIDER: Thanks.

LARRY: As you can see, that's the longest list, but there are a few things on our collective plates that we can't decide without you. We came up with a list of these, places where we really can't move forward until we have your input. I've put them in this column here. As you can see, there are six key items.

MR. AVOIDER: Okay, I'll take a look.

LARRY: Well, I appreciate how busy you are (Offers appreciation or understanding.), but we're all unable to go forward until we get some answers. Could we quickly go down the list and see what you can answer right now?

MR. AVOIDER: Okay.

LARRY: With the others, could you think about them and let me know at next Tuesday's meeting what you've decided? If we have a decision by Tuesday, we can keep these projects on schedule.

MR. AVOIDER: Okay.

LARRY: Thanks. We really appreciate that.

Larry then needs to follow up with an e-mail documenting the conversation and the agreed-upon dates.

Boss Communication Don'ts	Boss Communication Dos
Take your boss's behavior personally.	See things from your boss's perspective.
Expect your boss to fight all your battles.	Fight your own fights.
Give up on communicating.	Find a way to talk to your boss.
Put up with indecision.	Expect decisions.
Wait for your boss to meet for feedback.	Ask for a meeting.

Chapter 8

How to Ask for
Maternity, Sick Leave,
Disability Accommodation,
or Other Time Off

JOHN CHAMBERS SITS straight up in the middle of the night in a cold sweat. His skin itches, and his mind churns with the projects on his desk he can't seem to plow through. Depression has settled over him like a fog. He needs to talk to his manager today about some kind of time off or reduced workload, but as usual, the sense of shame at having a serious mental illness weighs him down.

John isn't the only person who can't sleep. There's a light on in Miriam Heller's kitchen, where she's trying, and failing, to read a book about breast cancer. Her doctor says her prognosis is good, but she'll be out of work at least three days a month for chemotherapy. What's crazy is that she's less upset about her health right now than she is about asking her Mr. Take-No-Prisoners supervisor for sick leave.

Across town, Chantelle Pickens sits in an overstuffed chair stroking her cat, thinking she'd be much happier to be up this late if she was feeding a baby. She and her husband have been trying for months, and today her boss caught her checking a site on how to tell if she's ovulating. The company laid off a woman just last year after she gave birth, and Chantelle is worried that if her boss knows she's trying to get pregnant, she might get laid off too. How can she protect herself from that happening?

Know Your Rights

Before you charge into your boss's office with a request for time off, arm yourself with your rights under the law, as well as your employer's policy. Be aware that some of the laws governing leave requests only apply if your employer has a certain number of employees, so be sure to check that first. Also, state laws create a whole different tangle of benefits, so research your rights in your particular state. Finally, if you're a union or government worker, those systems may create different benefits. This section is simply meant to give you an introduction and overview of this topic, rather than answers to your particular problem.

Family and Medical Leave

Under federal law, the Family and Medical Leave Act (FMLA), you have a right to twelve weeks a year of *unpaid* leave after your first year of employment with your organization to take care of a serious health condition, whether it's your own or that of an immediate family member. Denial of this leave is illegal under the Family and Medical Leave Act (FMLA).

You do not need to take this time off all at once but can do it in increments, as long as the total is no more than twelve weeks per year. If, for example, you need to take your husband for kidney dialysis every week, you would use one day a week of FMLA, up to twelve weeks total. In addition, you're actually entitled to a new twelve weeks every year. And, of course, you have sick leave and vacation time you can use first.

Disability

Disability claims in the workplace—both temporary and permanent—are skyrocketing and likely to climb higher due to changes in the law and aging baby boomers. Already, an astounding 75 percent of us will encounter some kind of permanent or temporary disability during our working career.

Most temporary disabilities will be handled under the FMLA or an employer's sick leave policies. If you have a more permanent disability, however, it's likely to come under the federal Americans with Disabilities Act (ADA).

If you have what the ADA terms a "permanent and substantial impairment of a major life function," your employer can't discriminate and must accommodate you. Accommodation can include time off and/or reduced hours.

If you are still able to perform your job with accommodations, and your employer can reasonably accommodate you without undue hardship, you have the right to be accommodated. Accommodations may include a special screen for your computer, a special

"We need to talk"

What is a *major life function*? Generally, the term encompasses things such as working, eating, sleeping, and walking.

chair because of back problems, or a flexible schedule for doctor's appointments. Time off may also be appropriate. If disabled, you may not be denied a promotion or job if you are able to do the work with a reasonable accommodation.

Mental health issues—substance abuse, depression, OCD (obsessive compulsive disorder)—should be treated the same as physical health issues if you have what's known as a "biologically based illness," but currently, state and federal laws create a tangle about this one. Your employer's health benefits may also dictate certain benefits. Check with your Employee Assistance Program in order to know your rights before you go in.

How Is a Reasonable Accommodation Requested?

In general, it's your job to inform your boss or HR that an accommodation is needed. The ADA jettisoned the old, paternalistic system that "employers knew best." This law assumes that people with disabilities know best what accommodations they need to be successful.

However, you can't expect your boss to read your mind and know that you secretly want accommodations, and then sue him for not providing it. As one court has noted: "The ADA does not require clairvoyance."

But the ADA does not mandate that you follow a formal procedure or use "magic words" either. Ideally, your boss should consider as a request for accommodation any statement saying that you need a job modification because of a medical condition that might be a disability.

If you've been on an extended leave, return to work, and then have difficulty meeting job standards, you may be disabled and need a reasonable accommodation. Before disciplining, terminating, or putting you on a performance plan, your boss should contact HR. They may begin a discussion with you about the appropriateness of a reasonable accommodation.

However, if your disability prevents you from asking for accommodation, and your boss knows about the disability and the need for accommodation, your boss can't ignore what he/she knows. As one court put it: "The employee may need an accommodation but doesn't know how to ask for it; the employer should do what it can to help." In my experience, most employers, as a matter of their own policies and values, try to do this anyway, but the law has made this mandate clear.

While most requests for accommodation will and should come from you, in appropriate circumstances—particularly if the impairment is psychiatric—a family member such as an adult child, or a physician, may make the request for you.

Employer's Duty

Once you've requested accommodation, your boss has a duty to engage you in an "interactive process" to determine the appropriate accommodation under the circumstance. An accommodation is not automatically reasonable if the boss simply agrees to the employee's request without an analysis of the worker's needs. In one appeals case, the employer agreed to a request for a modified work station because of a worker's carpal tunnel syndrome, but that accommodation was not effective and, therefore, not "reasonable."

On the other side, however, you have no right to compel your boss to provide a particular accommodation, if another effective, reasonable accommodation would work. And, the duty of reasonable accommodation is a continuing one. That means you have a right to request further accommodation as long as your requests are reasonable.

As your medical condition changes, as job needs change, or if you're transferred or promoted, your organization should re-evaluate your situation. If the original accommodation isn't effective, the interactive process starts again.

One employer, for example, learned this lesson to its chagrin in 2002 when it refused an additional accommodation to an employee whose multiple sclerosis had worsened, and fired her. The employee won $2,300,000 in compensatory and punitive damages.

Undue Hardship

Your organization only needs to make accommodations that are *reasonable*. What is considered reasonable is a question of the facts and circumstances of any particular case. Your organization isn't required to reasonably accommodate any disability if it would be an *undue hardship*. According to one company's lawyer, "As far as the government is concerned, spending money is never an undue hardship!" Buying equipment is almost always considered reasonable.

An undue hardship causes significant difficulty or creates a significant expense for the company site (not just your department) if it would "fundamentally alter the nature of the business." Courts look at the net cost after tax credits.

When the ADA passed, Congress recognized that hiring people with disabilities could cost companies more. Congress explicitly made the decision to shift the costs of supporting people with disabilities from the taxpayers, who pay the costs of a non-worker disabled population, to the employers who will get the benefit of the work they perform.

When the ADA was being considered, business lobbyists asked Congress to put a $10,000 limit on the amount an employer would be required to spend. This was defeated, so the courts have assumed from this legislative history that an employer could be required to spend more. However, according to a report from the Office of Vocational Rehabilitation, over half of the people with disabilities who were accommodated required *no* extra costs, and another 30 percent required expenditures of less than $500.

The same report found 91 percent of the disabled workers had average or better productivity on the job than non-disabled employees. 75 percent had better safety records. And able-bodied workers' turnover rate was 11:1 compared to people with disabilities. Most important to the issues of reasonable accommodation, 55 percent of the people with disabilities had better attendance than able-bodied workers, and only 5 percent had worse records. These are useful statistics to have in hand if you find your boss resistant to giving you the accommodation that you need.

Extended Leave Not Reasonable

If you have a disability and need more than the twelve weeks of leave provided by the FMLA, how much time off can you expect before it's an undue hardship? It depends on the answers to these questions:

- Is temporary help available?
- How essential are the job functions?
- How will work delays impact the company?
- How much time off is requested?
- Is the employee otherwise satisfactory?

The courts agree that, generally, regular and reliable attendance is an essential function of a job. Requests for indefinite leave have been uniformly rejected as unreasonable, since the purpose of accommodation under the ADA is to allow disabled people to work, rather than to hold a job for someone who can't work.

Other cases hold that employees who are unable to return to work after exhausting the one-year leave of absence provided for in company policy are simply not qualified to work and therefore, can be terminated.

In one case, the employee argued that her employer was required to accommodate her frequent absences by eliminating its leave restrictions, allowing her to take donated leave, granting her additional leave without pay, permitting her to take unscheduled leave as needed, letting her use compensatory time before she earned it, and having her make up absences before or after they occurred. The court refused, reasoning that allowing the plaintiff to work basically whenever she felt up to it was not a reasonable accommodation.

However, providing leave *within* the terms of the company policy is not an undue hardship. For example, in one case, two short leaves (two to four weeks each) due to flare-ups of lupus were not unreasonable, particularly since the employer took six months to fill the employee's position after she was fired. In another case that year, a worker's request for a short extension of her one-month leave for depression was held reasonable. And, in a third, the employer violated the ADA by rejecting a senior employee's request for sixteen weeks of paid leave, because company policy provided for up to thirty-nine weeks of paid leave for such employees.

In general, the courts have required more protection and accommodation for long-term employees. This is important to remember when you talk with your boss. Be sure to remind him or her of the length of your employment.

The courts have split on the question of whether employers must allow telecommuting as a reasonable accommodation. In a 2003 policy statement, the EEOC (Equal Employment Opportunity Commission) said that the ADA does not require an employer to allow a tele-work program, but if an employer does offer tele-work, it must allow employees with disabilities an equal opportunity to participate in such a program.

It's important to remember that neither the FMLA nor the ADA allows you to slack on performance. Within the bounds of whatever accommodation you've been allowed, you need to meet normal performance standards; otherwise, your boss would be discriminating against other employees.

Pregnancy Leave

The FMLA covers the birth of a child of the employee (mother or father), as well as the placement of a child with the employee for adoption or foster care. FMLA is unpaid by law. Your organization can deduct your pay, whether the employee is exempt or nonexempt, for all hours not worked as a result of leave.

You may elect, and your organization may require, employees to take all accrued paid vacation sick leave and personal leave during an FMLA leave.

The Federal Pregnancy Discrimination Act gives pregnant applicants and employees more rights than they had in 1978, when it was passed, but significantly fewer rights than employees protected by the Americans with Disabilities Act (ADA) and the Family and Medical Leave Act (FMLA).

During the first year of employment, employees are not entitled to family and medical leave. Nor does the ADA apply to temporary disabilities. So when the law says that pregnant applicants and employees "shall be treated the same as other persons . . . similar in their ability or inability to work," one group of workers they can be compared to is first-year employees with short-term disabilities.

Once employed, during the first year, pregnant employees must be treated consistently with everyone else. For example, a federal court of appeals ruled in 1994 that an employee who was excessively absent due to morning sickness could be terminated. The court wrote, "If an employee cannot work because of illness, nothing in Title VII requires the employer to keep the employee on the payroll."

A normal pregnancy is not considered to be a disability, but if you have to be on bed rest or be hospitalized, or you have other medical issues, you may qualify as *temporarily* disabled and be entitled to take time off under the FMLA, after your first year of employment, or under your company's sick leave policies. Since no pregnancy lasts forever (although sometimes it feels that way), you would not be entitled to protection under the ADA, which only applies to *permanent* disabilities.

Changes Coming to FMLA

The Family Medical Leave Act (FMLA) is undergoing change. The legislation was passed in 1993, and its first set of regulations was put in place in 1995. But court cases, including cases considered by the U.S. Supreme Court, have led the Department of Labor (DOL) to propose changes in the law that would solve problems that have arisen since that time, and problems surrounding a new amendment to the law. After more than six years of discussions with a wide array of stakeholders, not to mention more than 15,000 comments received since December 2005, the DOL circulated proposals for comments in 2008, with final regulations expected within the year.

More than 95 million people work for companies covered by FMLA, according to official statistics. Of that number, more than 77 million were eligible for family and medical leave, and almost 10 percent of those took leave, 1 million of them for intermittent periods.

Generally, strict rules apply for leave under FMLA, though they may be more flexible depending on the state you live in or the company you work for. Two conditions must be met for FMLA to come into play:

- Employees must have worked for a company for at least twelve months
- That company must have fifty or more employees *within a seventy-five-mile radius*

Under these circumstances, employees are eligible for twelve weeks of unpaid leave in every twelve-month period. Leave most often allows workers to care for newborn children, for family members who are ill, or for their own serious health conditions. The new proposals are designed to clear up ambiguities about how the regulations apply and the issues that have created problems between workers and their employers.

What's at stake?

Some changes are fairly basic and apply to both employers and employees. The new regulations will spell out more explicitly what is required for a worker to request leave if a temporary absence is involved. Among the proposed changes that are expected to be approved are the following:

1. **Employer's Response.** Once a request has been made for FMLA leave, an employer now has five days instead of two to respond, in a change designed to improve communication.
2. **Notice of Rights.** Employers will be required to give workers more explicit information on their FMLA rights. The changes will have to be included either in a firm's handbook or in an annual notice sent to workers.
3. **Disputed Documentation.** If employers find medical certification to be incomplete or insufficient, they must tell workers what information is required, and employees have seven calendar days to fulfill that requirement. The idea is to make sure that workers' requests are not denied on a technicality.
4. **Workload Changes.** Another proposed regulation will deal with issues that have arisen around "light duty." In the past, when employers have accommodated injured or ill employees by adjusting their workload or type of work, some employers have considered this as FMLA leave. The change is expected to make clear that this is *not* official leave.
5. **Paid Time Off.** Workers who take leave may also substitute paid leave, such as paid vacation or personal leave or other paid time off, either instead of or in combination with FMLA leave. Workers must first meet the terms and conditions of

the employer's paid leave policy but they are always entitled to unpaid FMLA leave if it applies to their employer.

6. **Access to Medical Records**. Changes would also streamline the content, clarification and timing of medical certification. Under new regulations, employers could directly contact health care providers as long as HIPAA conditions are met and as long as they don't ask for any information beyond what is included in the certification form.

Re-Certifying a Medical Condition

Under the FMLA changes, employers would also be allowed to request re-certification at least every six months, but not more than once a month.

So, for instance, Sue takes FMLA leave for cancer surgery and treatment. She asks for and is given six weeks of unpaid leave. Because the time period has been set and understood by both sides, the employer cannot ask for re-certification after only thirty days. But if Sue later requests an extra two weeks, the employer can ask to have her medical condition re-certified then.

Things are different for Joe, who takes leave for a specified period, but then asks his employer for three days a month for therapy or treatment for an indefinite amount of time. The company can request re-certification at that point and also in the future, if he is absent in excess of those three days per month for the same reason.

In order to take leave for a serious health condition, workers are not required to provide their medical records to their employers. In addition, all information that goes to an employer is treated as confidential and must be kept separate from normal personnel files. Also, workers are not required to sign a medical release as part of a medical certification. In order to return to work, you may have to submit a fitness-for-duty certification, even if your FMLA has been intermittent.

Military-Related Leave

The most significant change to FMLA is due to issues related to the wars in Iraq and Afghanistan and the resulting impact on members of the armed forces and their families.

In 2008, Congress passed an amendment to the act that recognizes the widespread incidence of severe injuries (such as loss of limbs and serious brain injuries) among returning soldiers, and the burden of care that this puts on military families. Certain provisions were put into effect immediately, but others need regulations in order for them to apply. The Department of Labor sought public comments during 2008 before it could fully implement these provisions.

The amendment provides two new types of leave. Both are extended to the families of service members in the armed forces, allowing twenty-six weeks of leave in a twelve-month period for the spouse, son, daughter, parent, or next-of-kin of a service member.

1. The first type of leave is designed to allow family members to care for servicemen and women who have suffered a serious injury or illness in the line of duty. The service member must be in medical treatment, recuperation or therapy; seeing a medical practitioner on an outpatient basis; or on temporary disability. This provision was put into effect in January 2008.

2. The second type has been proposed but is not expected to be ruled on until early 2009. It would provide twelve weeks for other conditions or situations that come with a call-up to

active duty. These could be child care, financial issues, or other impacts that affect families of service members.

Your Organization's Policies and Benefits

Before you go in to talk to your boss, be sure that you also know what your organization provides in terms of your company's own policy and benefits. These statements most likely provide even more than the law requires. If you're unsure, consult with HR or your benefits administrator (internal or external) first. You should also consult your organization's statement about what it values. Many organizations have strong statements expressing how much they value employees and how employees are their most important resources, and so on. While it's easy to become cynical about these statements, which frequently plaster the walls of corporate America, such statements can be helpful when used at the right time in a conversation with your boss.

Don't throw these statements in your boss's face, but rather try saying something skillful such as, "In thinking about my leave request, I reviewed all our policies and values, and I see that we specifically state that we want to value our employees' health above all else. I've always appreciated that statement and hope that it will guide us in sorting out this situation and help us come up with a solution that will work for everyone."

How and When to Bring Up Delicate Topics

Try to find out a time that's low stress for your boss—not, for example, the night before quarterly reports are due and everyone's running on empty.

Make sure you have a quiet room and his undivided attention: ask for an appointment ahead of time and give him an idea of how long you think it will take. Aim for less than thirty minutes; less than fifteen is even better. If you absolutely must talk to him by a certain date—your mom is scheduled for surgery, say—be sure to let him know that you have to talk by that time.

Come to the meeting armed with an understanding of the law and your organization's policy and values, but approach the entire conversation from a spirit of joint problem solving. Don't assume that he's going to say no or have a concern about a legitimate leave request. Go in with a positive attitude and plan that you feel will work for everyone.

How to Keep Your Cool During a Hot Discussion

Most bosses want to be sympathetic to requests for time off due to health-related problems, but if you are faced with a boss who isn't sympathetic or who is just plain ignorant about the realities of the law and your organization's policy, keep your cool. Remember the rule from Chapter 7: Don't take your boss's behavior personally. She may be ignorant of how leave requests should be handled or just plain mean for no good reason. Regardless, your job is to present your situation as clearly and logically as you can, stay as unemotional as possible, and then go over her head if you must.

Realize also that your boss may want to be sympathetic but may be worried about how she can get the work done or who will replace you if you take time off. Most bosses are stretched thin these days, with too much work and not enough employees. They may also have their own individual contributor work to do and not enough time to perform their management functions well. Work on not taking it personally.

How to Go Over Your Boss's Head if You Must

Be sure you have exhausted all your options with your boss before you move on. When you do decide that you have to go over his head, start with HR. Most good HR people these days are schooled in the ins-and-outs of leave requests and will understand what the company is required to do in a way your boss may not. If you don't receive what you need there, consult your boss's boss and/or an employment attorney. (See Chapter 4.)

Sample Script   *"We need to talk"*

JOHN: I need to talk to you about my situation.

MR. BOSS: Okay.

JOHN: You may have noticed that the work has been piling up on my desk, and I've been unable to get it to you in my usual time frame. I feel really awful about this and want you to know that I understand that this is unacceptable and that I don't want it to go on.

MR. BOSS: Yes, I've been meaning to talk to you about it.

JOHN: I need to let you know that I've been struggling with a personal health problem that's hard for me to talk about. I've had clinical depression off and on for much of my life. I receive treatment and medicine and normally, it's well controlled. I watch my health and as you know, I work hard to do a good job for our group. I want to continue to do that.

MR. BOSS: I'm sorry to hear about that.

JOHN: Well, yes, I've been dealing with it for a long time, so for better or worse, I've learned what I need to do to take care of it.

Right now my doctor has suggested that I go on a reduced workload of five hours a day so that I can get some extra treatment until I get my health back up to snuff.

MR. BOSS: Well, how long do you expect this to go on?

JOHN: I don't know for sure, but I think that it would be less than six months. I'm usually able to get things under control by then. I know how busy we are right now so I'd like to be able to make sure that we have someone to pick up the slack. I've done some research, and I have a list of freelancers who've done good work for us in the past. I'd be happy to contact them for you to see who might be available to pick up the slack until I'm back full time. Would you like me to do that?

MR. BOSS: Well, I think I can do it for you. I'm sorry to hear about your illness. I had a brother who suffered from depression so I know how hard it can be. You're a valuable employee and I understand that you need to take care of your health. Talk to HR about the paperwork and let me know if there's anything else I can do to help.

Here's another example of how to ask for leave for a serious medical illness.

Sample Script

"We need to talk"

MIRIAM: Mr. Attila-the-Hun, I've got some bad news.

MR. ATTILA-THE-HUN: I hope it's not another contract down the drain.

MIRIAM: Actually, it's personal. I've got cancer. (Cuts to the chase—shows that she means business.)

MR. ATTILA-THE-HUN: Whoa.

MIRIAM: Yeah. I found out yesterday. But the prognosis is good.

MR. ATTILA-THE-HUN: Glad to hear it. Sounds like it's not going to be that much of a problem.

MIRIAM: Actually, I'm concerned that it might affect workflow in the department over the next few months.

MR. ATTILA-THE-HUN: Because . . . ?

MIRIAM: I'll be undergoing chemotherapy and the doctor says I'll be out at least three days a month—or longer, depending on how my body responds to the treatment.

MR. ATTILA-THE-HUN: I'd say that's a real serious threat to the department's operation. And I really can't approve that kind of time off. I'm afraid you're either going to have to tough it out or we may be talking about a layoff.

MIRIAM: Actually, the head of Human Resources—

MR. ATTILA-THE-HUN: Don't bother with them. This kind of thing is up to me and I'll get back to you, as soon as I've had a chance to talk with Mr. Boss.

MIRIAM: I would love for you to talk to Mr. Boss about this. (Letting him know they're on the same team.) I know it's really a big deal to take this kind of leave. In fact, when I went to talk to Human Resources about this, the first thing they did was to go over company policy with me.

MR. ATTILA-THE-HUN: I really don't think that applies—

MIRIAM: (Speaking his language by interrupting him back.) I was so relieved to find out that the company does provide unpaid leave in my kind of situation. I gave HR all the particulars, and they've gone ahead and gotten in touch with my doctor.

MR. ATTILA-THE-HUN: Look, Miriam, I can't have people who don't perform. With the Glycol contract coming up for bid, this could have a very serious effect on the company.

MIRIAM: I agree. (Showing her loyalty to the firm.) That's why I want to work with you to come up with a plan to take care of this. HR says they expect to approve my leave this week, but you and I need to work out the nuts and bolts of how this works. Given how much I already know about Glycol, I think it's imperative that we start to come up with options as soon as we can.

MR. ATTILA-THE-HUN: Such as?

MIRIAM: I've already brainstormed several ideas. Here's a copy of a memo I've shared with HR. If you could look it over and think about what options seem best to you, I'll set up a meeting so we can nail down the details. I think we can get this up and running pretty quickly.

MR. ATTILA-THE-HUN: Well, I have to admit, you've done your homework. Enough said. Thanks for the effort. I'll take a look.

MIRIAM: I appreciate it.

Asking for maternity leave can sometimes be difficult. Here's a way to begin.

Sample Script

CHANTELLE: Hey, Ms. Unsympathetic, I've got a quick question on company policy that I thought you could help me with.

MS. UNSYMPATHETIC: Policy about what?

CHANTELLE: Maternity leave. I'm happy to say that I'm pregnant.

MS. UNSYMPATHETIC: Hmm. I guess congratulations are in order.

CHANTELLE: Thanks. I've talked to Human Resources, and I wanted to let you know that I've asked to go on maternity leave in September and to be gone for three months.

MS. UNSYMPATHETIC: Well, I wish you the very best. I'm sure it will all work out, one way or another.

CHANTELLE: That's what I'd like to talk about: how we're going to handle things while I'm gone.

MS. UNSYMPATHETIC: I don't think you need to concern yourself with that. I'm sure we'll find someone to pick up the slack.

CHANTELLE: I know company policy says that I could be transferred to another department when I get back.

MS. UNSYMPATHETIC: Yes, I'd say that's a definite possibility.

CHANTELLE: Can I tell you how I feel about this? (Makes a request.)

MS. UNSYMPATHETIC: Well, I suppose so.

CHANTELLE: I really love this job, and I want to make things work so that I can come back to it after my maternity leave. (Makes her feelings clear.)

MS. UNSYMPATHETIC: I appreciate that, but we'll just have to see what happens.

CHANTELLE: I want you to know that I'm passionate about what I do. I've got great relationships with my clients and they're really happy with my work.

MS. UNSYMPATHETIC: I hadn't heard about that.

CHANTELLE: How about if I ask Dale to drop by? He's head of the team and he can tell you all about the contributions I've made. And I'll forward the e-mail I got last week from the Piedmont CEO. He's really happy with how things have turned out. He says he hopes Piedmont can work with us again. (Makes a case for her own value to the company.)

MS. UNSYMPATHETIC: Okay, I'd be open to that.

CHANTELLE: I just want to add that if you end up hiring a contract worker for the three months I'm gone, I'd be happy to coach that person on any of my projects—until I can take up the reins myself when I come back. (Takes initiative but makes sure the conditions of her offer are understood.)

MS. UNSYMPATHETIC: That would certainly help. Let me think about it.

CHANTELLE: Great. I really appreciate that. I want us to keep talking so we can come up with the best resolution for the company.

Boss Communication Don'ts	Boss Communication Dos
Talk to your boss cold.	Do your homework.
Ignore your rights.	Insist, diplomatically, on your rights.
Leave your boss with no help.	Research temporary help.
Assume your boss will say no.	Go in with a positive attitude, seeking a joint solution.

Chapter 9

What to Say When You're Fired or Laid Off, or During an Investigation or Disciplinary Action

KATIE KLINE, FOR once, had no answer for her boss's question. "When would you like to get together to discuss handing off your cases?" he had asked.

Harry had just informed her she was being fired. "Terminated," was the nice word he used, but fired was the reality. She'd been in coaching for weeks—"charm school she called it"—for her "poor people skills" but she'd had no idea that termination was on the horizon.

Canned, fired, terminated—whatever—she had absolutely, positively no idea what to say!

Know Your Rights

Many of the legal principles in this chapter only apply if you're employed by an organization with a certain number of employees. Your rights may also vary depending upon which state you're in and

145

whether you're a government or union employee. What follows are the general rules. As is the case throughout this book, this material is offered as educational information, not in the context of an attorney-client relationship.

Termination

As explained in Chapter 2, you have a basic right under employment law, as well as good business principles and common sense, to be treated fairly. One of the consequences of this general principle is that you have a right to be given feedback about your performance and warned before firing. I always advise my clients that terminations should be "no surprise" to the person being fired.

Often, we hear what we want to hear, so even if we've been warned that if we don't shape up we'll be fired, we may not have really heard what we were told or believed that anyone would do anything at our particular employer.

> **"We need to talk"**
>
> It's amazing how often employees say that no one is ever fired at their organization. This may seem to be true, but many times what looks like a graceful exit may have been a forced departure negotiated behind closed doors.

If you're fired for poor performance, you should have been given the feedback that you needed in order to improve your performance, warned that you would be terminated if you didn't improve, and given a reasonable amount of time to improve. What's a reasonable amount of time to improve? Bosses should give employees at least as much time to improve as they would give a new employee to master the skill or task. So, if it would take a new employee six weeks to learn a new computer program, for example, the employee who is not performing well on that task should be given six weeks to improve.

If you're fired for poor performance without these warnings, it could be what's called a "wrongful termination," entitling you to sue for wrongful termination if you decide to take that tack. (More about this later on in this chapter.)

Terminations for theft, harassment, violence, or other misconduct can be done immediately. Obviously, if the behavior's severe, a manager, supervisor, or executive doesn't need to wait for the person to improve.

Consistency in Termination

Your boss must be consistent when it comes to disciplining and firing employees. They have to give the same level of discipline for the same type of misconduct. Your boss can't fire one employee for poor performance if other employees with worse performance aren't terminated.

The courts have also found a lack of fairness if bosses encourage employees to break a rule. Your boss can't turn around and fire you for that.

Firing employees fairly also means terminating them only if your boss has a legitimate business reason. You shouldn't be fired for what you say and do away from work, unless it affects your performance or your coworkers' ability to do their jobs.

In one case, for example, a salesman was owed commissions by his employers. The salesman kept doing his job and performed well. But he also filed a lawsuit against the company to collect his commissions. They canned him and he sued for wrongful termination and won. The court found that when an employee is terminated for a reason that's not related to his or her job, that's something outside the employment contract and makes the firing a wrongful termination.

> **"We need to talk"**
>
> You should be told the truth about your termination. Many times bosses fail to do this and give some excuse—such as the department's being re-organized. The courts have held that it's not fair to give an untrue reason for termination. This is especially true if you have an employee handbook. If, for example, your handbook provides for progressive discipline and your boss claims you were laid off, he or she has violated the employment contract as provided for by the handbook. The courts have found this to be unfair and a wrongful termination.

Confidentiality Is Key

Your boss should keep the reason for your termination confidential. Only other managers, supervisors, and employees—such as HR—who have a legitimate business reason to know, should be told. If more people are in the loop, you may have a case for defamation. In a Florida case, for example, a store manager told other employees that a twenty-year worker had been fired for dishonesty. The employee sued for defamation (saying something false about someone that injures their reputation) and won $200,000. At trial, the employer couldn't actually prove that the employee had been dishonest, so the employee won his defamation claim.

You should be fired in private, at an appropriate time and place. If you're not, you may have other claims if the firing is egregious enough. For example, a 2002 Colorado case involved a branch manager who was out on sick leave for a heart condition when he was fired, after twenty-two years on the job. The company sent two supervisors to the house where the manager was in bed, walked in uninvited, and announced they had his termination papers, which he needed to initial.

The managers didn't ask how he was feeling or if he felt well enough to talk with them. The VP who had ordered the firing told the supervisors, "I don't give a shit if [he] is on his deathbed, if I tell you to fire him, that's what you will do, or I'll get somebody who will." The manager tried to commit suicide that night. Not surprisingly, a jury awarded him punitive damages.

If you're terminated for cause—performance or misconduct— you won't be entitled to unemployment, but many employees go ahead and file, assuming that their company won't respond to argue about whether or not the termination was proper.

Layoffs

Layoffs are, unfortunately, common in these days of downsizing, right-sizing, and mergers and acquisitions. If you're over forty and have toiled for years in corporate America, you or someone you have worked with has most likely been laid off at least once. Under the WARN Act, the company must give sixty days' advance notice of a mass layoff or plant closing. However, the law applies only to companies with 100 or more employees and only to certain types of layoffs. Government or union employees may have even more rights in this regard.

In general, most courts will not second-guess layoffs or reductions in force (RIF), even if you think it's wrong, since employers have a right to make bad business decisions, as long as they follow the law when doing it. There are three areas where courts might find a wrongful termination:

1. If the layoff was in fact not legitimate
2. If there was no valid criteria for the layoff
3. If some groups protected under discrimination laws were adversely and disproportionately impacted

As to the first exception, if a laid-off employee is replaced within six months, the RIF looks suspicious. Courts will sometimes find wrongful terminations here.

Some companies have written policies that establish criteria for selecting employees for layoffs, such as seniority, job titles, or merit. All of these are legal as long as they're applied consistently and are backed by documentation. Criteria must be based on legitimate business decisions and should be in writing. If the criterion isn't applied consistently or could be viewed as discriminatory, a court might consider the termination wrongful.

Discriminatory Layoffs

If you believe that you've been picked to be laid off because you were over the age of forty (age discrimination), or because of your sex, race, pregnancy, or other protected characteristic, you may have additional rights to pursue.

Age discrimination, for example, is the fastest-growing type of discrimination case in federal courts these days, partly because of layoffs. What happens is that companies decide to lay off workers to cut costs. They start looking at the salary numbers and notice that older workers are the most expensive. Someone comes up with the bright idea to lay off the most expensive workers; they do and then seem surprised when they're hit with a class-action age-discrimination case. Workers frequently win these cases, especially if they're in a workplace—which is common—where there are lots of "jokes" about age.

Investigations

Second only to performance appraisals, investigations of complaints are the next area where courts have required your employer to be fair. If another employee has complained about you, or your boss has complained about your performance or behavior, your employer has an obligation to investigate before taking action.

Investigations are required for fairness because obviously, a complaint only highlights one side of the story. Your employer needs more information before they can take action. Your employer or your boss has an obligation to learn all the facts, especially your side of the story if you're being accused.

Your boss should be totally fair in conducting investigations. Anything she says or does that appears to be less than neutral, or that indicates bias or prejudice, can be used against her later.

Generally, the investigator should talk not only to the accused, but also to witnesses, and should be reviewing documents and going back to the complaining employee for more information.

If you're being questioned by your boss as a part of an internal investigation for misconduct, theft, harassment, discrimination, or other issues, the first thing to understand is that the rules in workplace investigations are different from investigations conducted by the police, and you have different rights.

Investigation Myths

Many times people assume that what they've seen on *Law and Order* governs workplace investigations and start asserting that they have a right to an attorney, a right to confront their accuser, and other such claims.

Not true. While employers are obligated to conduct internal investigations in these situations, different rules apply for workplace investigations than criminal investigations. If the misconduct could involve a crime, there may also be a parallel police investigation going on and, in that situation, the rules of criminal investigations would apply to the problem. But with workplace investigations, the standard is that your employer conduct a "full and fair investigation and come to a reasonable conclusion."

Your employer may even come to the wrong conclusion, as long as the conclusion is reasonable. An important Oregon Supreme Court opinion exemplifies this standard.

In that case, two women allegedly made violent threats against a coworker. The employer conducted an investigation; they questioned witnesses. The accused employees were informed of the charges against them, and the employees gave their side of the story. They denied making threats. After listening to everyone, the company believed the accusing employees and fired the two women.

The women sued for wrongful termination. They said they didn't make threats and that they could prove that they didn't, but the court at that point found their proof irrelevant.

The court said that even if the investigation turned up the wrong result, the company still couldn't be sued for wrongful termination as long as the company conducted a sufficient investigation; it acted fairly. The fact that it might have come to the wrong conclusion was irrelevant.

This standard is in contrast to criminal investigations and trials, where you must be found guilty "beyond a reasonable doubt." This is a very high standard, in contrast to civil disputes such as employment lawsuits, where the standard is "a preponderance of the evidence." What that means is that if there's some evidence on each side, you go with the side with the most evidence, even if it's just a feather's weight more.

During the investigation, you have a right to be treated with respect, even if you're the accused. You can be questioned but not interrogated. What's the difference? Well, if they lock you in a room with sixteen FBI agents and refuse to let you call your mother, you're being interrogated!

> ### "We need to talk"
>
> Your employer does have a right to ask you questions, and your employer's policies (reflected in employee handbooks or other documents) may contain wording requiring you to cooperate with any internal investigations. You can be disciplined or terminated if you fail to follow these internal rules.

Although you don't have a right to have an attorney present at work, you do have a right to contact an attorney on your own time. You may have a right, under a union contract, to have a union representative present. You also have a right to know what exact behavior you're accused of engaging in, as well as the exact policy or law you've violated. You do not have a right to know who accused you of this behavior, nor is there any Fifth Amendment right to confront your accuser. The Fifth Amendment only applies in criminal investigations.

Investigation Facts

If you believe that you were terminated without a full and fair investigation, that you were the subject of the investigation because of discrimination, or that your employer didn't come to a reasonable conclusion, you may have a right to sue for wrongful termination and/or discrimination.

You have a right to have what you say—as well as the entire investigation—kept confidential. Workplace investigations should be kept confidential; only people who need to know should know. If there's a lot of gossip about the investigation going around your workplace, you can and should complain. If the statements made about you to people who are not involved in the investigation are false and damaging to your reputation, you may have a claim for defamation.

General Rules about What to Say and Not to Say

While each situation is different, here are some general guidelines about what to say and do for terminations, layoffs, and investigations.

Don't get defensive. Obviously, this is enormously hard to do if you're being accused of something or have lost your job.

Ask for specifics. The devil is in the details, in this as in many things. Ask for specifics on your firing, any severance, or the details of the accusations.

Ask for time to respond. Ask if you can think about what they've told you or the questions they're posing and respond at another meeting.

Manage your emotions. Don't erupt, throw things, or blame your boss. He may have had little to do with the decision and may be your best ally in making lemonade out of lemons.

Negotiate. Ask for something, no matter how bad the situation. Ask for severance, ask for time to clear out your office, ask for them to talk to the people you want during the investigation. Ask for a referral letter or outplacement counseling.

Leave gracefully. You never know when you may be rehired or vindicated. Being a class act will always serve you.

All of these situations can be extraordinarily difficult, but if you try to stay calm and follow this format, your chances of having a good result go up substantially.

More about What to Say During Specific Situations

While the previous general rules will serve you well in most situations, some specific problems require different strategies. Here are a few examples.

Discipline

If your boss tells you that you're being disciplined, the first thing to do is follow the previous rules: Don't get defensive, and ask for details. Find out if it's a verbal or written warning, and ask for time to respond. Then, know your rights. Go back and look at your performance reviews to make sure that you've been warned if the discipline is for poor performance. If it's for other matters, ask for the results of the investigation and try to assess whether it's met the standard of being full and fair.

If you believe that other witnesses should have been interviewed—or if you have other evidence to present—ask for another meeting to present these suggestions.

Review any policies in your employee manual or website to find out if the company has followed its own policies in imposing discipline.

If you're a union member, contact your union representative to find out whether you have any additional rights under your union contract.

Investigations

Again, start with the basics: Don't get defensive, and ask for specifics. You have a right to know the exact accusations against you, although not the right to know from whom the accusation came. This is because most workplace environments are very public, and anyone could have seen the alleged behavior, not just the person or persons affected by the behavior.

Take notes. Document the questions asked and your responses. Ask to go get something to take notes if you don't have anything with you.

If you believe someone else should be interviewed, specifically ask the investigators to interview that person. If there's some other evidence in your favor they should review, tell them that also.

Ask for another meeting at the end of the interview. Tell them that you want to review the notes you've taken and get back to them if and when you remember anything else. Ask when they're going to get back to you and how long they anticipate the investigation will take. Ask what their standards are for conducting the investigation. Ask what the consequences will be if you are found to have engaged in the alleged behavior.

Layoffs

Again: keep your cool and ask for details. Ask what severance package they have in mind, if any. Ask if you can have the company pay for outplacement counseling. Ask for their cooperation in maintaining your health insurance, if you have it, through COBRA (Consolidated Omnibus Budget Reconciliation Act). Ask (although they may not be willing to tell you) for the details on the layoff in general—especially for information about others who are being laid off. Ask for a reference letter.

Termination

Once again, keep your cool and ask for details. Terminations, based on good practices, should not be a surprise. If the termination is the result of an investigation, ask for a copy of the investigator's report. Ask for the reasoning in coming to the termination. Document what they say and what you say. While you may think it odd to ask for something when you're being terminated, remember my basic negotiation rule that *it never hurts to ask!*

What kinds of things might you ask for? Here are some ideas:

- **A severance package.** Believe it or not, some employers do offer severance, even when someone is fired, as a way of trying to ward off lawsuits. Ask.
- **Outplacement counseling.** Could happen. It never hurts to ask.
- **A recommendation letter.** You never know, perhaps your boss is just the messenger and doesn't agree with the termination. He or she may agree to write you a letter.
- **The chance to clean out your desk in private.** Terminations should be done with dignity and respect. You shouldn't be marched out of the office with two security guards unless there's an immediate risk of violence to your coworkers. Ask for the time to do this privately if you wish.
- **Anything else you want.** *It never hurts to ask.*

When and How to Consult an Attorney

If, after reading all of this, you have any inkling that your rights have been violated in the process, it's well worth your while to consult an attorney.

Attorneys are very specialized these days, so find one who specializes in labor and employment law—especially someone who specializes in representing plaintiffs, meaning the employee. There are several resources in Appendix A, but you may also consult your state bar association or a local law school for referrals.

"We need to talk"

Most attorneys will do a one-time consultation for a set fee. Be sure to ask what the fee will be when you call to make the appointment. Once they decide to take your case, most plaintiffs' (employees') lawyers work on a contingency-fee basis. What that means is that they don't get paid unless you win, although you will have to pay for court and expert witness costs.

While you should never make up a claim, you should always assert your rights if you believe your employer has trampled on them. A one-time appointment with an attorney can pay handsome dividends in the end, or at the very least, give you the peace of mind of knowing that you gave it your best shot and you just need to move on and start fresh.

Sample Script

MR. BOSS: Katie, I need to talk to you.

KATIE: Yes?

MR. BOSS: I'm sorry to have to tell you this, but we're going to have to let you go.

KATIE: Really? I am so surprised. Could you tell me your thinking?(Asks for specifics.)

MR. BOSS: Well, you know that we've had problems with your people skills and asked you to undergo coaching, but we just haven't seen any progress in the last six months. You'd been given a final warning.

KATIE: I see. Well, I'm surprised. I liked working here and thought I was making progress.(Stays calm.)

MR. BOSS: I'm sorry too. I hoped it would work out.

KATIE: I would like to think about this and get back to you. Have you considered what kind of severance package you might offer?(Asks for severance and another meeting.)

MR. BOSS: Hmm . . . I don't know. I'll talk with HR. They may have something in mind.

Boss Communication Don'ts	Boss Communication Dos
Walk in unprepared.	Know your rights.
Lose your cool.	Stay calm.
Just listen.	Ask questions and take notes.
Go it alone.	Seek advice from your union or an attorney.
Take what they give you.	Ask for what you want.

Chapter 10

How to Tell Your Boss You're Quitting

MATT LEBLANC SAT in the bar with a partner from the D.C. office and a young Denver associate, complaining about his boss's hours. "I've been keeping track of Jim's hours: 10:00-12:00, then a long lunch, then he's out by 4:30. Nice life, huh!"

Matt's history of whining about his boss's incompetence, correcting him in meetings, and going around him to garner plum assignments finally caught up with him at his next performance review: "Not a team player" and "attitude problem" topped the negative list of problem behaviors. Matt could see the proverbial writing on the wall: making partner at the firm, not in this lifetime. He had to leave, but at least on his way out he'd have the satisfaction of telling his boss what he really thought!

Giving Your Boss Feedback

Whining about the boss tops the list of popular workplace activities. "Everyone does it," you might think, and that may be true. Like many things, however, just because everyone does it doesn't make it right. And more importantly, it doesn't serve you in the long run.

Venting is good: we all need a time and place to kvetch about a bad workplace situation, but find someone outside of your particular milieu: your best friend, a therapist, or priest. Constantly gossiping about your boss's foibles to anyone in your workgroup who will listen is neither gracious nor smart workplace etiquette.

If you're asked to fill out 180 or 360 surveys about your boss, as is popular these days, you may offer skillful feedback but make it constructive, not destructive. Although such surveys are usually confidential, your boss may be able to ferret out who wrote what, and destructive comments will come back to haunt you.

Make It Constructive

What's constructive feedback for your boss? Remember, as we discussed in Chapter 1, your job is to try to find out what your boss is trying to accomplish and help her do that. In truth, there are few bad bosses, just bosses that you're not managing well.

If you've found out how to help your boss and get her what she wants, she's likely to think that you're great, and a boss that thinks you're great will help you get what you want—different assignments, travel, more or fewer hours, and so on.

If you must give your boss feedback, make it constructive, meaning that you are behaviorally specific (see Chapter 2) about things that are within your boss's power to change. Whining about things that she can't change will not serve you. Ask, for example, for more specific feedback on your work, not for a promotion that you know your boss has no budget to give you.

When to Leave

If you've tried all the other conversations in this book in the hopes of making your workplace situation better, and you still find that your job and/or your relationship with your boss is intolerable, then it may be time to leave. It's always better to leave than to spend your days miserable in a job where each day you feel as if you're gulping a teaspoon of poison.

As said before, the reality is that your boss is your boss for one and only one reason: someone above him thinks he should be the boss! He's not your boss because he's the smartest or best at his job or because he necessarily has the best management skills. In an ideal world, of course, these would all be qualifications, but this is not an ideal world. Your whining about your bad boss is unlikely to change his behavior or your place in the organization. In fact, the opposite is most likely to be true: you will develop a reputation as a whiner and a back-stabber. Trust me; these are not resume-building attributes.

"We need to talk"

Be wary, however, about quitting to make yourself happy. All the happiness studies show that making more money or creating the perfect new product doesn't make you happy. Happiness comes from relationships and the opportunity to do creative work. See *The Geography of Bliss: One Grump's Search for the Happiest Places in the World* by Eric Weiner and *Stumbling on Happiness* by Daniel Gilbert.

If you have no control over your work, your work doesn't allow for any creativity, or your commute takes hours, these things can make you unhappy, but your work alone will never make you happy.

Finding a new job, however, can help you build your resume and start fresh. Having the ability to quit and quit well can give you a sense of more stability and help you see that you have the ability to get a new job when you need one. The people with the best skill sets have the most flexibility when it comes to changing jobs. That means you have to be building your skill set constantly. If you're in a job where you're not able to learn constantly, try to get on a project that will challenge you or ask your company to pay for training (easier to do if your boss thinks you're great).

Time to Leave
When do you know that it's time to move on? Take this test:

- ✓ You honestly do not have a bad habit of leaving jobs at the first sign of conflict or difficulty.
- ✓ You've diligently tried all the tricks in this book in order to improve your chances of loving your current job and managing a difficult boss.
- ✓ You're constantly miserable.
- ✓ Your mental or physical health is suffering because of your job.
- ✓ You're being subjected to mental or physical abuse or harassment.
- ✓ Your spouse, best friend, significant other, priest, and/or therapist is telling you that he or she can't stand to hear about your crummy work situation one more time.

If you agree with and check off two or more of these statements, it's time to move on.

What if You Feel Bad about Leaving?

While it's true that it's an employee's market these days, most people at the bottom can be easily replaced. If you have a good boss, they probably know that you're looking. Many younger employees are often looking for new employment opportunities—that's why the busiest time on Monster.com is just after lunch on Mondays!

Unfortunately, your company has little loyalty toward you. If you were to be laid off, you could be shown the door with as little as two weeks' notice. If your boss or some other mentor has been good to you, don't leave them in the lurch by letting them spend months trying to get you a promotion and then leave. But you don't owe them the advance warning that you're looking until you have a new job. Until you quit, there's nothing that they can do. Telling them just creates more stress for the both of you.

What if they try to get you to stay by offering you more money, better hours, or work-at-home options? Think about all these things before you quit, so that you know your own bottom line.

What to Say and What Not to Say

Don't burn bridges; they're hard to rebuild. Most industries track members, and your words will come back to haunt you. Be gracious when you leave. Simply announce that you've found a better fit for you, no more. Don't take a last opportunity to trash your boss. Don't go on the company blog and burn the organization. Clean up any messes before you leave. The odds of your words or deeds coming back to you like a boomerang are astronomical in the age of the Internet as well as industry conferences, meetings, and other corporate swap meets.

Also, you never know when you might want to return. A change of bosses in your group, or a change of heart for you, could easily drive you back into the arms of your former employer. The wise and successful consulting company, McKinsey and Company, has accepted this essential truth so thoroughly that they actually have clubs and newsletters for McKinsey alumni. They know that the name means something and smart employees take advantage of that boomerang effect.

"We need to talk"

When you do sit down with your immediate boss, think of something positive to say, something that they gave you that you're grateful for. Everyone has strengths and weaknesses; try to find your boss's strength and focus on that.

Negotiating Severance

Sometimes when you leave a job, you may be able to do so with your pockets full of money (or at least a check). At a minimum, you may want to research using all your sick leave and vacation time. Also, be sure to find out whether your health insurance can stay intact if you're going to be unemployed for some time. A federal law called COBRA (Consolidated Omnibus Budget Reconciliation Act) requires employers to offer you the option of keeping your insurance (monthly premiums paid by you) for some period of time. You might also want to explore any other legal right you might have through a one-time consultation with an employment attorney.

Employment law, as with most other areas of the law, is quite specialized these days. Because employment lawyers specialize in representing plaintiffs (employees) or defendants (employers), you need to be sure to find someone who specializes in plaintiffs' employment law, preferably as all or most of his or her practice. Ask your local bar association or the National Employment Lawyers Association (NELA, *www.nela.org*) for a referral.

Legal Options

If your employer has trampled on your legal rights, however, you may want to explore your options. What other legal claims might you have? Discrimination or harassment, of course. Be aware, however, that generic bad behavior or a personality conflict with your boss is not discrimination or harassment. You need to prove that your boss or coworkers treated you badly because of your age, race, sex, disability, sexual orientation, and so on. There is an overview of many of these legal claims in Chapter 4.

You may also have a claim for *constructive discharge.* This term describes the outcome of a situation in which a boss wants to terminate an employee but is afraid to fire him or her, so the boss starts treating the employee badly by changing the work schedule or assigning undesirable work and difficult or impossible-to-reach deadlines. The employee then gives up and quits. Instead of suing for wrongful termination, the employee sues for constructive discharge, which means that your situation at work has become so intolerable that a reasonable person would quit.

Many times these kinds of claims do not require an actual lawsuit—a potentially career-ending move in some industries in which everyone knows everyone else. (And, of course, with the Internet these days, future employers may track down your history of claims.) Instead, an attorney can simply advise you of your rights, and you do the negotiation on your own. Alternatively, an attorney may negotiate an out-of-court settlement for you before any lawsuit is ever filed.

If you think anything close to what's been described here may be happening to you, it's well worth your while to spend the money for a one-time visit to an attorney. Find out ahead of your appointment exactly what you will be charged for this visit. You might also want to call the local bar association or any law schools in your area to determine whether there are any free or reduced-fee clinics available to you.

Sample Script

"We need to talk"

MATT: Jim, do you have some time right now to talk? It's important.

JIM: Sure.

MATT: I just wanted to let you know that I've decided to move on to another opportunity. I wanted you to know before anyone else. I also wanted to thank you for all I've learned in working with you about transportation issues. I've really appreciated your patience in describing all those complex regs to me. (Appreciation or understanding.)

JIM: Well, this is a surprise. What will you be doing?

MATT: I'm going to be working on Brown's legislative staff on environmental transportation issues. It's a field I've always been interested in pursuing and this opportunity just came up.

JIM: Well, that does sound like a good option.

MATT: Yes, and I wanted you to know that I'm sorry for my contribution to our differences in the past. I suspect that I'll see you at future Board hearings and I just want you to know that I've learned a lot about how to give people feedback. I realize that sometimes I was out of line.

JIM: Well, I can see how we both contributed to that situation, I wish you the best.

MATT: Thanks. I wish you and the organization the best also. I've prepared a list of the things that I've been working on with suggestions for next steps and who I think might know enough about the issues going forward. Let me know if there's anything else I can do to clean things up before I leave.

JIM: Thanks. I'll take a look at it and let you know.

Boss Communication Don'ts	Boss Communication Dos
Trash your boss.	Give your boss constructive feedback.
Burn bridges.	Leave with diplomacy.
Stay if you're miserable.	Leave if you must.

Chapter 11

How to Cope with Difficult Workplace Feelings

GERRY FALDMAN NEARLY broke out in hives every time he walked in the corporate entrance. He had officially accused his boss of harassment after enduring months of tirades and a devastating performance review. He had spoken with an attorney and carefully taken her advice, proceeding one step at a time, and the company was doing a full investigation now, including interviewing his coworkers. As he sat down in his cubicle, he could feel himself start to sweat. He had no idea what others were thinking about him or what they'd told the investigators. It was awkward, to say the least. He was afraid if he so much as struck up a conversation with anyone, he'd be viewed as trying to intimidate or manipulate them. He didn't know how he'd make it through another day on the job.

Bouncing Back

Whether you're screwing up your courage to ask for a raise or facing a Nightmare Boss every day or you think you might be going to court over a workplace issue, you could be wrestling with some pretty big emotions. Feelings are part of the human equation, and there are times that all of us—from the lowliest intern to the top dog in the executive washroom—have to cope with how we feel. How you handle this part of the business "conversation" can be a make-or-break deal, which means it's important to manage both the inner and outer part of the game.

I used to work with the former president of the Colorado Bar Association. Originally, she practiced criminal defense and had worked as a public defender. She joined the firm I was working for and began doing civil work, primarily in employment cases. After she'd been there a while, I stopped in to see how she was doing and asked what the difference was between doing criminal defense and doing civic work.

"My clients are so emotional," she said. This surprised me and I asked her to explain. "Criminals are so used to being accused, it's just no big deal." In contrast, our firm represented corporate cases—managers, executives, people making lots of money—who were deeply upset because they had been accused of harassment or discrimination. People don't like to think of themselves in that light, and it makes it a hundred times worse when it becomes a public and legal accusation. Meanwhile, the emotion on the other side can be just as intense. The plaintiff has been traumatized by harassment and nobody believes them, making it even more traumatic. Now they're caught in the court system, which is enough to traumatize anyone.

Getting Through the Tough Times at Work

Even if the issue is just that you want to lead the next big project or you're waiting to hear on a promotion, you are likely to have feelings about it. Of course, jitteriness doesn't help and can even amp up your anxiety to the point of disaster. There you are in the break room, acting nonchalant with the boss, when you suddenly realize that your fly is down, you've just let slip some wisecrack, and your coffee mug is taking a nose-dive for her new silk suit.

There are important things you can do to manage your emotions and keep yourself on an even keel, no matter what the challenge, but as I've said in other parts of this book, it's also crucial to cultivate your understanding of the boss, of her strengths, and of the pressures inherent in the situation.

One factor that compounds communication at work is that bosses are authority figures and their roles are sometimes parental. That by itself doesn't mean they have the necessary skills, time, or energy to nurture your career, to mentor you or even to listen to you, to hear you and see you clearly—never mind addressing your needs. This is true whether they love you or couldn't care less about anyone they supervise. The most important thing you can do is to depersonalize the situation and anything that's said with regard to it. You know you've got a problem if you find yourself replaying scenes from childhood dramas, whether you're doing it on the job or lying in bed at night thinking about work.

Separating Your Feelings from Workplace Issues

To deal with emotions around a challenging job situation, try taking stock of who you are and what baggage you bring to the situation. Your real task in life is to take care of yourself: You render unto Caesar what belongs to Caesar, and the rest is all yours. No matter what the issues are that you're facing, your job is part of a business, and it's imperative that, as much as you possibly can, you park your issues at the door, separate your emotional needs from your financial ones, and give your best rational thinking to your work.

Let me be clear: I'm not suggesting at all that you suppress your feelings. You ignore them at your own risk, because your feelings are the keys to recognizing what's really true for you and what you really need. By the same token, you don't let yourself break down sobbing or fly into a rage in the middle of your presentation to the board of directors. That's the kind of thing you do in the safety of your own home, with a friend, or in a session with a therapist. By separating your feelings out like that, by taking action to open your heart and vent your feelings on your own time, you have the reward of clearing your mind. This way, you're not dragging your frustration or disappointment into the office and letting it sabotage you.

> **"We need to talk"**
>
> The more you can move out of the realm of emotion at work, the more likely you are to see the situation for what it really is and be able to make rational decisions based on that information. When feelings aren't clouding your thoughts, your brain will function at a higher level. Not only will you see the situation more clearly, you'll see what's under your feelings: the unrealistic expectations you've been harboring about your boss and about yourself.

You could discover that you've been thinking the boss should know how good your work is, even though she barely has time to read her own e-mail. You may figure out that for your entire career, you have been driven by a kind of perfectionism that has a dark side of resentment and bitterness. Or maybe you'll find a pattern of trying so hard to prove yourself that you end up undermining your efforts and then self-destructing.

The point is that once you have insight into the underlying causes of your feelings, it becomes easier to handle them and you're less likely to feel them so deeply or to stay stuck in them. Bringing them down to a manageable level will increase your chances of success in dealing with your current challenge. That will also help you manage all the other arenas of your life, which are probably affected by whatever situation you're faced with.

Catching Up with Yourself

Not yet convinced that it's important to deal with your softer side—or that you can? Not even convinced that you have a softer side, or that it matters? Or maybe you're afraid that once you go there, you're going to dissolve in a puddle of tears and never recover. Sure, you can tough it out, grit your teeth, and "get over it." But will that help? Do you really think you can make those feelings go away?

Even if you work hard at suppressing them, negative emotions can eat you alive. They can wreck your health, your relationships, and your state of mind. And they're not that much fun to live with, either. If you're coming home cranky or depressed every day, whining and demanding attention from your friends, and bitching to your teammates on the basketball court, well, is that the life you had in mind for yourself?

When it comes to your health, studies have shown that bad feelings sustained over a long period of time can be extremely destructive. Researchers have found that chronic anxiety, anger, or depression actually fuel changes in your body—and the news is not good. Your risk of contracting an illness or worsening an existing condition goes way up when you're locked in bad feelings and you stay that way. Scientists have documented the emotional link to diabetes, heart disease, and high blood pressure, among other health issues. A Harvard School of Public Health study released in 2007 even suggests that emotion plays a role in triggering heart attacks.

> *"We need to talk"*
>
> On the other side of the coin, positive emotions do all kinds of good things for your body, from repairing the damage done by stress to making your immune system more resilient to disease, not to mention improving your mood, your parenting, and your outlook on life.

Depending on the degree of difficulty of your current situation, the very idea of feeling happy right now may sound impossibly goody two-shoes—you might as well try to be Julie Andrews in *The Sound of Music*. How, you say, can I possibly feel good in a situation that is so bad?

When it comes to managing negative emotions in tough situations, let me reassure you on two counts:

1. It may not be easy.
2. It's absolutely essential.

Your emotions change your brain and your body—for better or worse. They can make a bad situation impossible, or they can help you cut your losses and start feeling safe again. They can support you as you rebuild your life or cause you to spiral down into debilitating, self-defeating behaviors.

Wondering how in the world you can find a way to leave that Looney Tunes supervisor behind and find places that crank you back up into feeling normal and human and worthwhile again? Try out a few of the following strategies to get beyond that feeling of being sentenced to round-the-clock hard labor and dizzying disappointment.

GOOD HEALTH, GOOD TIMES

There are reams of literature on how to lift your mood and deal with bad times. The top three recommendations on most lists are exercising, eating healthfully, and getting enough rest. These can be a challenge all by themselves during a hard time—but they're worth every ounce of effort. Just throw some fruit and veggies in the shopping cart (and then, of course, eat them). Make sure you get three meals a day, and minimize the white stuff (sugar, white bread, etc.) and remember that emotion is what lies behind the drive to eat a bag of cookies or drink yourself into oblivion. If you figure out the feelings that are under that desire, the impulse is likely to evaporate or at least scale way back.

Exercise will also help clear your head and, at the same time, give you an outlet for anger. If you leave work wanting to kill someone, try finding a gym and a punching bag. How about a grueling session with the treadmill? Or just take it out on a pillow when you get home (this can get pretty vigorous, depending on what happened at work that day). Visit a batting cage and imagine the ball is your boss, then hammer it over the fence. Do the noon calisthenics class at the local Y—that can't help but relieve some of the pain. And, as an extra bonus, exercise can help you sleep at night.

At the same time, be reasonable about your own limits. If you wake up crying every morning or can't get to sleep night after night, it's time to get some professional help. See your doctor or a psychiatrist and find out what they can prescribe for your current condition. The right medication can go a long way toward steadying you through this time.

A Little Help from Your Friends

No question that your best buds are on your side and ready to back you up. Your role? Don't wear out your welcome. Spread the wealth: When you need to talk to someone about something that's just happened, think about choosing someone other than your best friend, if that's who you've called night after night for a week. Don't burden anyone with complaining; just get the reassurance you need to know that you're okay out there in the world—and then move on. If you know that you'll need continuing support, it's important to maintain your network of friends by being considerate of their feelings.

But how about those friends you've got at work? It's another resource, no question. But on the job, you're colleagues; you're not there to hang out. It's well known that friendship at work brings greater satisfaction to what people do, that it creates better working relationships and even increases productivity. It also gives you more staying power. Human resources research indicates that the number one indicator of longevity in a job is whether an employee has a best friend at work.

While having a friend in the office can be great, it doesn't give you free rein to bad-mouth others or complain about your situation. The cold, hard truth is that you have a profession, and you're expected to be professional about it. That's key to communications in the workplace and to keeping your situation as self-contained as possible. Spreading negative feelings at work can easily backfire and make you look like the bad guy, whereas restraint can earn you other people's respect, as well as your own.

SPUR OF THE MOMENT
Just got turned down for the raise? Told the promotion went to someone else? Did the Boss-on-Wheels make yet another demand?

Maybe it's time to plan a vacation, listen to music, or suggest to your spouse that you take in a film after work. Meet a friend for coffee and see if you can talk about almost anything else but work. Go for a long walk, admire the scenery, and give a smile to at least one person you pass. Buy flowers and bring them back to the office to cheer you up all afternoon. Sit in your car and just scream for as long as it takes to get past those nasty feelings. Almost anything you can do to get out of the office and away from that moment will help, as long as it's not self-destructive. Don't let the emotion hurt you any more than it already has.

CHILDHOOD MOMENTS
Got kids somewhere in your life? There's nothing like a bout of rug-rat laughter to make your day. Little ones can help you find a way to pull yourself out of the doldrums and get yourself into the present moment, which is where children live all the time. Reading a story to a tiny tot or reading together with an older child can get you back to the times in your own life when stories made you feel good. And hey, why not stop at the library on your way home from work? Harry Potter never hurt anyone, and neither did *The Wind in the Willows* or *Dune*. You can also go the grown-up route: I bet

there's a John Grisham or a Stephen King that will keep you up all night—but in a good way (and hopefully, on a night when you don't have to be on the job the next day).

Smile Your Troubles Away

Research has shown that positive emotion and a hopeful, optimistic attitude can improve health, that in fact it is so powerful that it can even help increase the chance of surviving cancer. But did you know that smiling—just making yourself smile—can bring into play the same neural networks that are triggered by spontaneous moments of joy?

In the 1990s, Dr. Paul Ekman, a psychologist at the University of California at San Francisco, coauthored a study that indicated people can bring on a pleasant mood simply by making their facial muscles move in a certain way. His research suggests that there are techniques for us to produce our own emotions, even if it's just a subtle change in mood, and that this can bring on a more positive outlook on the world or even evoke good memories from the past.

Remembering When

The brain can't distinguish between what's happening right now and a memory of something that happened in the past, so during a tough period, one thing you can do to support yourself is to write down pleasant memories, as many as possible, and then visualize one or two every day. Re-imagine the wonderful things that happened, feel the feelings of that time in your body, and let your senses relive that moment. The brain will take it from there. Creating an internal video loop of positive memories can help you keep your head above water, even in the toughest times.

Keep 'Em Laughing

Another way out of the pit of despair is what's called Laughter Yoga. This sounds like something straight out of *Reader's Digest*, but Dr. Madan Kataria, a Bombay physician, has discovered that laughter really is the best medicine. He developed this particular kind of yoga by teaming traditional yogic breathing exercises with full-out laughter. Initially, he was at a loss for how to prescribe such treatment—the breathing was one thing, but it wasn't like he could send people to a pharmacy to buy bottled laughter. Instead, he hit on the idea of creating Laughter Clubs, where people go to laugh. (Don't laugh! It's true.) There are now more than 5,000 clubs in more than fifty countries. (Think what this could do for world peace!) Some have even been established in workplaces, and others have demonstrated the process at schools, governmental agencies, hospitals, hospices, and even military and police installations.

The idea of a global NAFTA-type agreement for humor may not hit your funny bone just right, but Kataria has a really interesting take on all this. Laughter isn't just silly or frivolous, he says, but a way to get at the deeper meaning of life. And if we reserve laughing only for the good times, we miss the boat. It's important to learn to laugh over our difficulties and failures, too, he says.

Maintenance Is Key

Keep it up—all this support adds up after a while. No one thing is going to float your boat, so make a habit of boosting your mood. Keep a journal. Take a class on communication skills. Find a support group or someone who can help—a pastor, a priest, a rabbi, a counselor, a life coach, or a psychotherapist. Draw or paint. Take a long bath with candles and Kenny G. Try out a kayak. Hang with your homies or go to church or temple. Take refuge in solitude or at a concert or on an iPod bike ride. Watch a movie. Watch two—make them both comedies. Take in the sunset or call a distant friend or a favorite relative.

"We need to talk"

Does doing all of this mean that you'll win? That you'll get promoted, earn that bonus, or get that incompetent lout called your boss thrown out on his can? There are no guarantees. But separating your work life from your emotional life can't help but make things easier.

You probably already know what kind of toll this problem is taking on you and on your personal life. And you probably feel that you've got to do something to stop that. Intervene early and often.

My point is this: There are ways to nurture yourself that you might not think about if your work situation has become an obsession. There may be good reasons that you're so upset, but it's not helpful to stay keyed up all the time. Think about letting go for a while, shifting gears into something more comfortable, something that feels good. What happens at work stays at work—where it belongs, and where it won't stew your goose, make you miserable, and drain away any zest for life that you ever had. The pain of your everyday work situation may not be going away anytime soon, so why let it take over your entire life? Acting on your own behalf can make you feel more powerful and keep you on an even keel. It can also give you your best shot. And a best shot is worth having, no matter who you're talking to.

Going for the Gold

Most of the ideas in the previous section are how-to-get-through-a-tough-time techniques. They keep you steady while you decide what your next steps are. They're important. But the very best strategy for dealing with any of the situations described in this book is to identify your own passion and to figure out your own goals, what's really important to you and what you need most.

Looking through photo albums and petting the kitty may soothe you for a while, but they can't help you cope long-term if you've got a boss who reams you daily just for kicks.

You may need every last skill in this book, but the most helpful one is to find yourself. There's no better time than a crisis to figure out what you truly need—not just what you want out of the situation and what's possible, but your purpose in life. The question of where you go from here shouldn't be so much about desperately plastering your resume on Monster.com. It should also be about dreaming big and strategizing about how to start making it happen. If you can see your way clear, this tough moment can be an opportunity to find out what will make you happy in the most profound sense of that word.

But hey, if your goals aren't really that lofty at the moment, let's be honest. Maybe you're less interested in maintaining a professional attitude than you are in seeking revenge.

If you really just want to tell someone to "take this job and shove it," you can do that. The question is: Will it advance your career? Get you a job recommendation? Keep you fed and warm and sheltered? It's your choice, of course. But chances are when you get done blasting the entire management team off their Herman Miller chairs and after you've sniggered and chuckled and laughed your head off about it and shared your moment of glory with every last one of your buddies, you'll be faced with the task of paying your mortgage and buying your kids' shoes.

It may be tough to take, but the truth is: This is business. It's not about you; it's about getting the job done. And while you deserve to be respected in the workplace and to absolutely fight for that, you may have some bitter pills to swallow anyway. Whether they have legal ramifications is an issue you will have to work out with an advisor, such as an attorney. But be prepared for the worst: This whole crisis may simply turn out to be one of life's great disappointments, something you have to chalk up to experience and then come to terms with.

"We need to talk"

Best advice: Maintain your dignity, stay professional, and if you find yourself with a pink slip in your hands, go out with class. You never know when you might be rehired or find a job through your old connections.

What to Expect if Things Get Legal

Some of the situations covered in this book can be overwhelming and the remedies can be drastic. If you're just asking for a raise, the rest of this chapter may not apply to you, because the level of intensity just isn't the same as when you've got a higher-up talking about why you need to have sex with him or when your ethnicity has become the object of jokes and ridicule. Under those kinds of circumstances, things can get out of hand pretty fast.

Though federal regulations allow you and your employer to settle issues yourselves, in some cases you may find that legal help and legal action are your only choices. This can add to the stress already in your life. It may feel like insult added to injury, and it could cloud your judgment or even embitter you. Those support strategies become more important than ever when the ante goes up and you find yourself shutting down emotionally or raging at the dry cleaner on a regular basis.

Working Out a Settlement

It can be harrowing to consult with an attorney and find that you do not qualify to take legal action against an employer that you feel has injured you. This may happen if you failed to document the harassment you endured or failed to report it to the proper authorities, or simply because the law doesn't cover your particular case.

That doesn't mean you have no leverage. Employers may recognize that the situation has been harmful to you and they may wish to make amends. Or they may believe that they are liable to some extent, and they may hope to avoid dealing with legal claims, which can be expensive to settle.

How do you determine what legal claims might you have?

Sally, for example, walked out when her boss tried to change her longstanding work schedule. Because of health problems, she'd always worked four short days. Her new boss basically took a take-it-or-leave-it attitude. "This is the job you have," she sniffed.

On my recommendation, Sally consulted an attorney who analyzed her situation under the Family and Medical Leave Act (FMLA), which provides that under certain conditions employees have the right to take up to twelve weeks a year (unpaid) to take under certain care of their own health situation or the health problems of their immediate family members. (See Chapter 8 for more information on FMLA.) Employees are not required to take the twelve weeks all at once, as long as they can document the need to take portions of the leave at different times.

Sally's attorney also analyzed whether she had any partial disability claims. Though the attorney was unable to determine the issue for sure, she helped Sally draft a letter outlining her concerns and advised her to request one from her employer.

In a panic, Sally called her attorney in the middle of the negotiations. "I'm afraid that they'll think I've talked to an attorney if I say what you've suggested," she cried.

"So?" responded Ms. Attorney.

"But then it will turn into a confrontation."

"So?" repeated Ms. Attorney.

"But then they might get upset at me!"

"So?"

You get the picture. Taking this tack may require nerves of steel and some outside coaching, but Sally pulled it together and waltzed away with a severance package that allowed her four months to determine what she wanted to do next.

Legal Proceedings

Worst-case scenario, you end up talking to a lawyer under the most serious conditions possible. "Talk" suddenly takes on a whole new meaning. Going to court or engaging in attorney-represented negotiations is one of the most challenging "conversations" there is. The kicker is that it needs to be done by other people on your behalf. In other words, you have to stay out of it.

Most employment cases are settled in-house. They may involve attorneys either as consultants in the background or in direct negotiations. As I recounted earlier, in the story about the former criminal defense lawyer, these cases are unusual for attorneys. Legal representatives will tell you that such situations are dominated by emotional issues, and that the feelings loom much larger than any legal outcome that either the plaintiff or the defendant is seeking.

Workers who believe they have been harassed often want nothing short of public humiliation for their current or former employer. The individual who is accused in the case may fear the loss of his reputation, as well as the end of a long career, unless the employer is formally acquitted. These expectations bring an unusually high charge to the case.

The first steps your attorney will take are to investigate your claims and identify the legal issues in them. Your deposition is likely to be the most important document in the process, because it will determine what kinds of documentation are necessary to back up your claims.

"We need to talk"

It is your words that start things off. They educate both your attorney and the opposing side about the issues in play, about responsibility for the situation, and about the potential damages. If this is a strong enough statement, backed up by enough documentation, it may force the other side to sit down and start settlement talks, instead of going to trial.

Settlement will involve mediation. You are likely to be offered an agreement that will involve both financial issues and other matters, with terms that lay the foundation for a final settlement. There will be release forms that your attorney will explain to you. Monetary terms will not only involve a total figure of the settlement but also how and when the money will be paid.

Chances are there will not be an admission of responsibility on the part of the employer, and your attorney may counsel you about this, since it could be a grave disappointment. It is, of course, just one more trying emotional moment and one that is crucially important to come to terms with when it comes to writing the settlement agreement, because no one wants the issue to come up in the final conference. Other issues may include asking you to resign or to agree not to re-apply for employment; giving you letters of reference; making disposition of your retirement funds; getting you to agree not to make negative statements about the company or its employees; and guarding the company's trade secrets.

Any of these issues can raise your emotions. But a settlement is just that, just like sediment settles to the bottom of a river. Once you've talked it over with your attorney and your family, friends, or counselor, you need to either come to peace with it or come in with a counteroffer. And once there's an agreement, you really have to let it go. Let it finally be over and done with.

Keeping Your Cool in Court
It is unusual for employment cases to go to trial, but it does happen. And now we're talking about top-of-the-line stress, whole new layers of it, as well as complications to your life that you never

dreamed of. Oh, and, yes, just let me mention that there are no guarantees that things will turn out in your favor—even if you win.

Your attorney will explain the ins and outs of the process to you, but one element is notable and may affect how you view the procedure. In some states, if your case goes to trial and you win, but the amount of the judgment is less than or equal to the settlement offer you were given, you will not only get only that amount of money, but you will also have to pay the court costs incurred after the offer was made. The process by which this figure is reached could make it include attorneys' fees as well. Not exactly cause for rejoicing.

So you see that an employment case is simply not a cut-and-dried affair. There's a lot of gray area. And if you keep looking for "windfall justice," you may be seriously disappointed, despite how your case is handled. As if this were not enough, the series of events you will be required to go through bring their own brand of stress. Just going in and out of the courthouse every day, whether or not Mr. Mike-in-Your-Face local TV reporter has become interested in your case, can be a trial of its own.

How do you handle it?

You've got to up the ante and redouble your efforts to support yourself. It may sound corny—like something you've heard in an after-school special—but paying attention to the fundamentals in life can be a saving grace in a situation like this. Beware of taking refuge in old standbys like too much beer, too much TV, or too much sleep. If you can't walk into the courtroom feeling at least a little refreshed, with a strong stride and the confidence that comes from feeling good and feeling good about yourself, chances are you will not make a very good showing.

What to Say and What Not to Say

It is possible that you will be in contact with the people you feel have injured you by harassment, discrimination, or retaliation. Your attorney will coach you on proper behavior in such instances, but let me make clear that no matter how strong your feelings, they simply do not have a place here. This is not *Judge Judy*.

Given that emotions are already running high, you need to find ways to restrain your impulses and to value your self-control. If you let your feelings get the best of you, you could very well hurt your chances of achieving a settlement.

Do the same as you've been doing up to this point: Take your emotions home, take them to a sympathetic listener, take them to your physician—find help anywhere you can. If you let them contaminate what has become a legal situation, you risk losing everything—and I mean that.

You may feel that you are owed, that you are right, and that you deserve not only your day in court but vindication in the local news media, if not national newspapers. Remind yourself that you are up against a powerful opponent but that you also have resources. Remember how far you've come and how much you've endured. And above all, treat yourself with respect. You deserve better than a fistfight in the halls of justice.

Sample Script

"We need to talk"

GERRY: Susan, I wonder if I could have a few minutes to talk with you.

SUSAN: Well, I'm pretty busy right now . . .

GERRY: I promise not to take more than five minutes of your time.

SUSAN: Well, okay. But just five minutes.

GERRY: Thanks. I appreciate it. I just want to check in with you. I really appreciate the way we've worked together in the past, and I want you to know that that's still true for me.

SUSAN: Well, yes, I guess I have to say that the same has been true for me in the past.

GERRY: I understand. And I also have to tell you that this investigation is making me feel very isolated. I don't want to talk to you about the issues connected to it, but I wonder if we could have coffee this week and just hang out a little?

SUSAN: Wow. I'm not sure about that. I'm afraid it might give people the wrong impression.

GERRY: I can see how that might be true. Let me just tell you what I've talked to my other work friends about—I'm asking how they feel in this situation. Would you be willing to share your feelings with me?

SUSAN: Gerry, this whole thing scares me. I don't know how I'm supposed to act.

GERRY: Man, I feel the same way. It's so awkward. And listen, I don't want to make this harder for you or anybody else but, boy, I sure could use a few friendly faces every day. Would you be willing to be one of those people? I just need a smile, a "Good morning," someone to ask me how it's going just in the social sense of the term, things like that.

SUSAN: Oh, of course, Gerry. I'm sorry I've been a little standoffish. It's been hard for me to know how to handle all of this. But if that will help, I'd be happy to do it.

GERRY: I'm really grateful for that, Susan. Thanks. I think this will really make a difference.

Workplace Emotions Don'ts	Workplace Emotions Dos
Lash out at your boss.	*Allow the process to work itself out.*
Let emotions eat you up.	*Separate emotion from other needs.*
Gossip with coworkers.	*Maintain neutrality and ask for appropriate support.*
Demand "justice."	*Request a reasonable settlement.*

"We need to talk"

Conclusion

By now I hope you've realized that conversations with your boss are not traumas to be feared or conflicts to avoid, but a chance to create workable solutions to joint problems. After reading this book, you should have the three things that you need to solve challenging conversations: the right attitude, the dialogue skills, and the ability to stick to your workplace goals and objectives.

Whatever your issues, great workplace relationships are well worth the investment. There are few things in your work life that will offer more payoffs. Everything that you want and need for a happy and productive work life is available to you through good conversations with your boss: promotions, salary increases, additional training, and other benefits. What it takes is your ability to reach out, create good dialogues, and manage conflict productively. Don't be afraid to step up to the plate and make these relationships work for you. You'll be glad that you made the effort.

Life is much too short to be miserable at work. One of the keys to creating a happy work life is having great working relationships with your boss.

I wish you well on your journey.

Appendix A

Additional Resources

9 to 5, National Association of Working Women
www.members.aol.com/naww925

American Civil Liberties Union
www.aclu.org

American Federation of Labor–Congress of Industrial Organizations (AFL-CIO)
www.aflcio.org

Asian American Legal Defense and Educational Fund (AALDEF)
E-mail: *AALDEF@worldnet.att.net*

Equal Employment Opportunity Commission (EEOC)
www.eeoc.gov

Mexican American Legal Defense and Educational Fund (MALDEF)
www.maldef.org

NAACP Legal Defense and Education Fund, Inc.
www.naacp.org

National Employment Lawyers Association (NELA)
www.nela.org

National Organization for Women (NOW)
www.now.org

Legal Momentum
www.legalmomentum.org

Salary.com
www.salary.com

Working America
www.workingamerica.org/badboss

Appendix B

Bibliography

Eisaguirre, Lynne. *The Power of a Good Fight.* Indianapolis: Literary Architects, 2006.

Gilbert, Daniel. *Stumbling on Happiness.* New York: Knopf, 2006.

Goleman, Daniel. *Social Intelligence: The New Science of Relationships.* New York: Bantam, Reprint Edition, 1997.

Hallowell, Edward M. *Connect.* New York: Pantheon, 1999.

Weiner, Eric. *Geography of Bliss: One Grump's Search for the Happiest Places in the World.* New York: Twelve, 2008.

Index